JESUS EQUALS LOVE!

Joel Wright

PREFACE

This book was placed on my heart by Jesus to share His truths and the realities of who He is and to help give a better understanding of the great depths of His love by expressing His grace, love, forgiveness, and dedication toward us. His love has inspired millions of people over the years. This book is aimed to help show some unique qualities of grace and the way God can transform us by His Holy Spirit. A song that has stayed with me is by Bill Gaither called "Something Beautiful." I find it has a perfect summary of the gospel of love, who Jesus is, and what He can do in our lives. There's a digital link below to this beautiful song that I highly recommend you listen to before we start.

Gaither Vocal Band - Something Beautiful [Live]

The lyrics share that Jesus can give hope in a life that was once broken and full of confusion. He can give us understanding by His working power of grace. We often only have issues and not much to give Him with our sorrow, but with His leading and directions, He certainly can pave a way for us that reveals to us beauty in a life once full of turmoil and pain.

INTRODUCTION

This book will cover the greatest love story, which is still in the midst of being revealed. This book will cover grace and mercy, peace and wisdom. This book is aimed at anyone in the faith or not. It will first start with simple foundational truths and then lead into the deeper processes of the Holy Spirit and how He does the work of grace within our hearts. It's aimed at growing your spiritual roots deeper to know Jesus so you can become a disciple of love. There will be many biblical stories that we will explore together that reveal God's personality and hopefully reveal a glimpse of His grace within your life. There is truly love on each page of the Bible when we search for it and gain understanding of His treasures.

My aim is to enable growth for all. We are in all different stages of our journey, and helping our minds be renewed into Jesus's image of love is the best way of starting our walk so we can do the good, perfect, and acceptable will of God. This book will cover some of my personal experiences of His grace that is always working and His colourful love that expresses harmony between brothers and sisters. Jesus knows a thing or two about sin and the wicked hearts of man. He reveals His tender mercies to those of us who have been in captivity to sin, and He changes us indelibly by His grace.

Thank you, and I hope you enjoy your journey with me in *Jesus Equals Love*. Let the transformational power of His Holy Spirit equip us for every good work.

Joel

Dedication

To Jesus Christ, the one who gives life and reveals the truths of His reality in this world that offers new understanding to those who believe the Gospel of Love.

"'Get wisdom! Get understanding!
Do not forget, nor turn away from the words of my mouth.
Do not forsake her, and she will preserve you;
Love her, and she will keep you.
Wisdom *is* the principal thing;
Therefore get wisdom.
And in all your getting, get understanding.
Exalt her, and she will promote you;
She will bring you honor, when you embrace her.
She will place on your head an ornament of grace;
A crown of glory she will deliver to you.'

"Hear, my son, and receive my sayings,
And the years of your life will be many.
I have taught you in the way of wisdom;
I have led you in right paths.
When you walk, your steps will not be hindered,
And when you run, you will not stumble.
Take firm hold of instruction, do not let go;
Keep her, for she *is* your life."

(Proverbs 4:5-13)

"'The fear of the LORD *is* the beginning of wisdom,
And the knowledge of the Holy One *is* understanding.'"

(Proverbs 9:10)

TABLE OF CONTENTS

CHAPTER 1

Nature Reflects His Personality

When I was young, I always loved to be outdoors. You literally could not keep me indoors! As I grew older, things changed. I became less interested in the outdoors and became more introverted in many ways. A life that was once full of fun, sun, and excitement became a little duller in my older years through playing computer games and being in my own little world. But it's not what God had destined for me, being inside and neglecting the living world that He had created for me to enjoy and to see His realities!

When I became born again, I finally understood what salvation was and how Jesus had died for me on the cross for my sins. Even though I already understood the concept of the cross, I did not understand the intensity of His love and grace or how Jesus needed to become as sin—treated so from the Father on the cross as a substitute for me to atone for my sins.

He gave me a new heart of love from His Holy Spirit. He gave me a new life, an eternal life. I am now able to know who created this fantastic world, and now He wants to talk with me? Out of nearly eight billion people, He wants to speak to me? But not only me, but He also wants to have a renewed, restored relationship with all the world if we will only let Him? I'm amazed at the intimacy Jesus can give us in our daily walk when we come to the knowledge of Christ and learn of His ways. He is so real and apparent when we learn to hear His still inner voice and leadings so we can become aware of His love and presence as a friend, protector, Lord, and creator!

God is long-suffering with all of us. He wants us to experience His very best for all of us to become transformed into His image, which is love. We will come to Christ's long-suffering and forgiveness in different chapters, but for now, I want to share with you the connection He desires for each one of us.

He can share His holy presence with us some may describe it as like a tingling electricity hovering over our being, or some may call it "goosebumps or shivers," but it's Jesus's power that is watching over us to encourage us and comfort us! He also shares His plans of love for His creation through His spoken word. Jesus is skilful with how He draws us near to Him, how He sees the best in us, and how He gives us His qualities of love through His Holy Spirit!

We were once in the fallen nature and sinful ways; now we can become love and His other characteristics, which God has enabled us with in the renewed man. That new man is given to us by the power of His Holy Spirit and the regeneration of the Word of God working in our hearts. It doesn't need to be complicated, as I'll explain in the next chapter! You will soon grow in grace and the work of love Jesus does in our hearts if you accept who He is and let Him transform your character into His likeness.

When I was baptised in the Holy Spirit, something changed in me. I knew I had been given the Holy Spirit in a way that God had initially intended for us to have Him. Like how Adam and Eve had God's glory upon them in the garden of Eden. He created Adam and Eve to know them on a personal level, to enjoy life, and to share precious moments with. He wanted to give Adam choices and let him name all the beautiful animals God had planned to share Adam's newfound world. God was so excited to share with His creations and to be able to share fellowship with His creations, which would be His delight and joy.

We were initially created to be in union with the Godhead, to be joined together in harmony, peace, security, and understanding that God is in control. There would be nothing more blissful than the utopia God had planned for His creation and for them to be in natural unseparated harmony.

Shortly after I received the baptism of the Holy Spirit, I went outside. I had a new perspective on life. Things seemed different; the sun was brighter, the clouds were more delicate, and the sky was full of life. The flowers had a hint of love with fragrances only an intimate creator could have formed in His superior wisdom and knowledge. For the first time, the birds were singing sweeter. I noticed the finer things of this world. It was like the Holy Spirit had opened my senses to the realm of His beauty and characteristics.

I often say to look at God through His creation: The blissful nature of rainforests. The gentle flowing trickle of a crystal-clear stream. The sun reflecting off the water ripples, like a diamond that sparkles! There are so many fine details in this life. We can see different and unique aspects of God's personality everywhere. He is the creator of, well, everything! He has the knowledge and the understanding to form life as we know it.

"For since the creation of the world His invisible *attributes*
are clearly seen, being understood by the things that are
made, *even* His eternal power and Godhead ..."

(Romans 1:20)

In the Bible, we can see glimpses of God's personality
through the knowledge He shares with us. He is wonderful;
Jesus is a creative genius. Think of how He has designed
every aspect in this world to the microscopic cells of a blade
of grass. It is almost out of this world in terms of
craftsmanship; it's an art, yet it's a functional power plant on
a micro-scale. It's amazing to be able to create such blissful
designs that flow in harmony. It is incredible how plants are
shaped and formed and how life's energy sources are
interconnected: the power delivery of the sun that uses
nuclear fusion billions of miles away, which becomes fuel for
the complex sugars and acids to be made. This is the
creator; this is our God. He is skilful and a master at what
he does. If we reflect on His personality, He is an engineer
at heart, a mathematician, a nuclear scientist, and a
gardener. And this is just a tiny microcosm of who He is ...

"When He marked out the foundations of the earth,
Then I was beside Him *as* a master craftsman."

(Proverbs 8:29-30)

His invisible attributes are in everything. Who decides the
way a flower appears in bloom? Was it not Jesus? As an
artist fashions a painting, does it not come from His heart to
show the beauty that is within? We must allow Him to open

our eyes to the reality of this world. The more we see His creation, the more we can see His personality and His creative work. He is the Great Artist. As a swift delicate painter's brush shares a story, it leaves indelible marks. Like a thumbprint that is always unique, it reveals our creator's immortal heartbeat in tune with life because He is life. As we admire His handiwork, God's characteristics reveal the essence of life through the designs!

Often the Bible mentions Jesus interceding in gardens when He was on His mission of love. Why do you think He went on journeys to find a place of prayer? To find somewhere quiet, perhaps? Not only quiet, but to be around the Father's creation, to be closer to the Father's attributes of order. The Godhead— the Father, the Son and the Holy Spirit— is the source of life.

The gospels reveal to us Jesus's personality more than anywhere else. He was inclined to pray in a soothing and quiet environment: a refreshing garden that mirrors heaven's attributes of peace and tranquillity. We see Jesus's love for nature and how He spent time with the Father in His secret place away from the rush of thousands following Him. He would often meditate on the Scriptures and express His prayers of love to the Father for His disciples that they may be strengthened for the fight ahead. He would share His feelings about His sufferings and what He was going to go through on the cross, to seek refuge for strength for what was needed to do the Father's will.

It is good to see how Jesus was relatable to us and how He managed His busy and stressful life by surrounding Himself with nature. He can teach us how we can take refuge in His peace and how He can lead us to meditate and pray in a place of tranquillity and be refreshed spiritually and physically. Jesus also describes Himself as being humble in heart (see Matthew 11:29). We can also see that Jesus is described as the Word of God (see John 1:1-14). He created everything we have come to know and love! Our beautiful world is from His masterful designs. So I can easily say we can see His characteristics through nature itself; at essence, God is life, so ... He gives and creates more life!

> "'I am the resurrection and the life.'"
>
> (John 11:25)

His creations are alive! Everything has a form of electricity flowing through it, from insects to birds. It's all energised as we discussed in the mechanics of a single blade of grass. The reason why I want to put into perspective a blade of grass and its inner workings is this: He can design intricate details on the most micro scale, and there are millions of cells are in a single blade of grass, ten quintillion insects in the world, and fifty billion birds alive right now. So it's not that hard to see that out of just less than eight billion people, He knows us by name, even down to the very hairs on our heads. You may say, "How is that possible?" But let's look at the complexity of Christ's creation in numbers we may find hard to understand: the vastness of the universe!

For example, the Bible says God has numbered all the stars. To us mere humans, that seems ridiculous, and we probably would have trouble naming one hundred stars before we ran out of unique names. Research suggests there are around two hundred billion trillion stars. For perspective, there are just thirty-two billion seconds in one thousand years, and I say "just" with a cheeky smile on my face.

"That's 200,000,000,000,000,000,000,000 [stars]!

"The number is so significant, it's hard to imagine. But try this: It's about ten times the number of cups of water in all the oceans of Earth."[1]

"He counts the number of the stars;
He calls them all by name.
Great *is* our Lord, and mighty in power;
His understanding *is* infinite."
(Psalm 147:4, emphasis added)

"'Are not five sparrows sold for two copper coins? And not one of them is forgotten before God. But the very hairs of your head are all numbered. Do not fear, therefore; you are of more value than many sparrows.'"

(Luke 12:7)

Do you feel humbled by those numbers? Maybe inspired, or it's too hard to comprehend? I feel you, but I wanted to give a ridiculous yet accurate stat that we cannot comprehend. I wanted to provide us with an understanding of how big God is and how small we are … yet the Bible verse about the sparrows shows us our worth and reveals the love He has for us. We are valuable. We are His creation, and He cares for you and me.

---

[1] Brian Jackson, "How many stars are there in space?" Sept. 20, 2021. *The Conversation:* https://theconversation.com/how-many-stars-are-there-in-space-165370 *(May 16, 2022).*

Are we not made in the image of God? How much more valuable are we than birds if we are made in His image? He is God; it's no small thing for us to be created in His image. We are the first created in His image—not even the angels were made to look exactly like Him. God has a unique plan for us to be shaped into love, and we will cover in the majority of this book how God's love is revealed to us and through us.

CHAPTER 2

The Likeness of His Image vs the Sinful Man

Since we can see an artist's personality through designs, how much more can we see God's through His living creation made in His image as humans? Well, not the fallen human nature we are acquainted with, but rather the renewed man made in love by the Holy Spirit. That is one way we can see the Holy Spirit at work in believers' lives: by the renewing and refining of our characters. It's the fire of the Holy Spirit that can burn off the dross and past ways of our life's sins and enables us to be purified as gold that is refined in the furnace. It's a process the Holy Spirit starts in all believers' lives to be transformed into Christ's image.

As I mentioned briefly before about the baptism of the Holy Spirit and fire, when we are baptised into His death, He starts the inner working of His Holy Spirit to set us apart for His use in His kingdom.

My born-again experience came at the same time as my baptism of the Holy Spirit, but I am not saying you need the baptism of the Holy Spirit to be saved. I believe the Bible teaches us to seek the baptism of the Holy Spirit for empowerment, equipping of ministry, boldness, and giftings (see Acts 1:5, 19:2-8). We are saved through grace from faith given to us as a free gift when we first believed and repented of our sins (see Acts 10:43). But the baptism of the

Holy Spirit and fire is a supernatural experience that sensitises us to the Holy Spirit.

With that awareness comes a holy lifestyle and an awareness of God's presence that supercharges the spirit man, which enables His children into full discipleship and allows them to be transformed for the work of His ministry. I believe that the Holy Spirit's inner working of His holiness and love toward us is to refine us as fire purifies gold: fire draws out all the impurities to ready us to be yielded vessels of honour for the Lord. That is what Jesus does. We must seek after the empowerment of His Holy Spirit in our lives to be further equipped and strengthened by the Holy Spirit. Let's take a quick journey back to Adam and creation, when God made man into His image. There are some simple biblical truths I believe are often overlooked that have key aspects for us to understand our walk of faith with Christ. Let's explore!

"Then God said, 'Let Us make man in **Our image**, according to **Our likeness**; let them have dominion over the fish of the sea, over the birds of the air, and over the cattle, over all the earth and over every creeping thing that creeps on the earth.' So God created man **in His *own* image**; in the image of God He created him; male and female He created them."

(Genesis 1:26-27, emphasis added)

When God created us, He destined for us to be like Him; we are in His "likeness" (Hebrew word *demuth*, pronounced dem-ooth'). The word likeness in Hebrew describes resemblance, shape, manner, and similitude, according to Strong's Concordance.

He wants our being to be like He is, but unfortunately, there has been wickedness of the human heart since our fall from God's holiness (see Jeremiah 17:9). We have our own free will to choose good or evil. We have been in a fallen state since Adam and Eve chose to rebel. The corruption of our flesh through allowing sin in the world often reflects the opposite of God's character or a jaded perspective of good because of the choices that we have allowed to corrupt us.

God never wanted us to have a fallen nature. He gave Adam and Eve a commandment not to eat the fruit of the tree of knowledge that revealed good or evil. It was not in His will for us to fall away from God's holiness and the relationship we had with Him because of our knowledge of right or wrong. Ultimately, their understanding took away their innocence once they knew they had sinned.

Adam and Eve chose to go against the command, and that direction was now set. As we are made in the image of God, we are not robots. God made a creation that loves with a free will. To have an authentic relationship, a willing relationship, we must have free choice, and that is why God has given us a choice to know Him or not. If we want to know good or evil and if we choose evil, there will be judgment, but if we choose to have faith in Christ, there will be atonement, meaning a remission of sins (they are taken away) and a relationship restored to the Father through Christ as our mediator. I know this may seem simple to some Christians, but it's so essential to share the simplistic truths of the gospel, to lay the foundation of love Christ set, so we can build upon and gain understanding to move into the full maturity of the Word and we can progress in our spiritual journey.

Jesus gave us a moral law of what is right or wrong. He placed that within our hearts after the fall so we can rule over sin (Genesis 4:7). Since now we have the knowledge of what sin is because of the fall (see Genesis 3:7), we now understand we are in need of mercy because the fallen flesh is swayed to corruption. We all know something is not right with the world, and its sinful ways and issues of life are often germinated from the root cause: sin. That is where the key of love can open hearts to understand an aspect that the world can overlook through the hardness of a sinful heart. His love has been with us to protect us and to guide us into the knowledge of what He did for us if we will only listen! (See Hebrews 3:15.)

He enables us to grow in grace once we understand our old rebellious heart toward God. We can be assured that He is loving to be able to provide us with many chances after the constant rebellion of humankind. We know He has the best intentions for us (see John 3:17), and just like the multitude of stars He created, He works above our understanding. Sometimes people can be upset at God because of pain and suffering in this world, but I urge you not to allow your limited understanding and past hurts to try to stop a rewarding relationship with Jesus. He heals the broken hearts and builds trust.

"'For My thoughts *are* not your thoughts,
Nor *are* your ways My ways,' says the LORD.
'For *as* the heavens are higher than the earth,
So are My ways higher than your ways,
And My thoughts than your thoughts.'"
(Isaiah 55:8-9)

Christ wants to give all of us His grace, and in His grace, we can come to the knowledge of His judgments and corrections. Sometimes pride and rebellion try to undermine our belief in God's knowledge of the greater good He has for His creation and the mystery He has revealed. Even though life is painful at times, we must look to the promises that meet the desires of our hearts. It takes humility and an open heart to see God's ways. Once inside His grace, you will never look back! Please take this journey with me to see how love is the key that opens the mysteries of life and lights up the paths to His kingdom that awaits!

"Did you say mystery, Joel?" Yes, I did, and I will cover one of the mysteries that God has had for us, well, since creation.

You may be thinking that's a bold proclamation. Yes, it is, but it has been revealed not only to me but to everyone willing to seek His treasure out. First, let's dig a little further for the treasure before the reveal ... Let's start with some basics, and then we will get into a deeper understanding of His love in different areas. It's always good to refresh our perspectives on His plans and to see His grace whether we are new or mature in Christ.

Our fallen nature has been revealed from our sin. Man has borne the consequences of that which ultimately leads to death, for all have sinned (see Romans 3:23). Jesus understands that death for mankind must happen because of the commandment given to Adam, which allowed death to enter into the world because all have sinned (see Genesis 2:17 and Romans 5:12-19). The Bible talks about how the final judgment is after death, once we have passed to the eternal spiritual realm and the world has been judged. We will all stand before the great white throne of judgment (see Revelation 20:11). Hopefully, we have chosen to accept faith in Christ to avoid the great and final day of judgment so we pass into eternal life and for all evil to be dealt with forever.

Jesus knows this life is just temporary, and He wants the best for us in eternity. It's not always just about this life we experience here; He sees a greater depth to life, and He wants to share it with us. He knows the best direction for us and the eternal home He wants us to choose. Sometimes as humans, we can be short-sighted—me included—and only think about this world without looking ahead in faith to the one that is much better than this one. We have opportunities to take the world that lies ahead and to invest wisely now for the eternal rewards.

Let's dig in on the quest for love. With the knowledge of Christ, we have escaped fiery judgment by His grace. We can be beneficiaries of love. Let's look at the judgement and how it leads to grace. Judgment is a good thing if we think about it in our society. If there is no justice, how hard would it be to live in peace? It would be chaos, and there needs to be justice for the injustices done. It seems fair, right? God has set a judgment for all sin, either in our minds or our physical actions. God is holy and just. It's a good thing for a day of sentencing if crimes have been committed—well, usually, unless we are the ones who are guilty. Then we are biased.

So, you may ask, "Joel, why are you explaining to me judgment and death in a book of love about Jesus?" Because this is the simple gospel of why we need the saving work He does in our lives (if you have not placed trust in Christ yet). It's wise to be open to God's plan for us, so He can show us love in so many ways. This book could never explain it all, although I will try on a broader scale to cover who He is, His mission of love with the inner workings of His Holy Spirit, and His character to help build on the foundation of the gospel.

CHAPTER 3
The Mystery Revealed In Christ

To understand the mystery of Christ, we must understand what is needed to be redeemed. It's our souls for eternal life and in God's grace and mercy that gives us a second chance in this life and opens the door to come through adoption into His family, to be called the sons and daughters of the living God. Adam was called the son of God because God created him. We are the sons and daughters of Adam's seed naturally through conception. Since Adam was tainted by sin because of his disobedience, we have fallen too.

God wants us to crucify our old man, spiritually speaking, his or her desires from the old ways of the fallen nature. You may say, "Joel, how do I crucify the old man?" Or you may say, "I am a believer. How can that be applied?" This is what this book will cover on an overall aspect with allowing the Holy Spirit to lead and direct our lives. By doing so, we'll hate the sin that we choose to do and turn from ungodliness and seek Christ's qualities by being transformed by His love.

He enables us by His Spirit to have a renewed heart toward God and to love people the way God wants us to, but in time, we are all appointed to die, and with death, new life will be brought in. We will be made eternal into the likeness of Jesus Christ if we live in the new man and are found in the faith of Christ. Jesus has given us a new life: the Holy Spirit within us when we repent and believe that Jesus is Lord.

"'The first man Adam became a living being.' The last Adam *became* a life-giving spirit.

"However, the spiritual is not first, but the natural, and afterward the spiritual. The first man *was* of the earth, *made* of dust; the second Man *is* the Lord from heaven. As *was* the *man* of dust, so also *are* those *who are made* of dust; and as *is* the heavenly *Man*, so also *are* those who are heavenly. And as we have borne the image of the *man* of dust, we shall also bear the image of the heavenly *Man*."

(1 Corinthians 15:45-49)

As part of entering into the kingdom of God, the Bible talks about how we must be born again in our spirit. Jesus Christ, who lived a blameless life and obeyed all the Father's commandments, achieved that ability for us. Jesus paid for our sins on the cross so we can be pardoned by a gift of faith that God gives to us if we choose to let Him into our lives. Now this is simple, but it's the gospel that is effective! So as Christians, we are to share and sow seeds of this grace into people's hearts. God wants us to share a simple gospel of love, one laying down their life (Christ the innocent) so we can enter our eternal home with God. The gospel is love, peace, joy, and hope. We are to be promoting love first, and this is where God's craftsmanship can come in.

> "For we are **His workmanship**, created in
> **Christ Jesus for good works**, which God prepared
> beforehand that **we should walk in them**."
>
> (Ephesians 2:10, emphasis added)

When we have an intimate relationship with the Holy Spirit, He moulds us to imitate Him, which starts when we first believe. When that happens, we are newborn babes in Christ. The real journey is where we go from there and how we can grow to bring more people into the kingdom of heaven. This is getting closer to the mystery that God has revealed.

> "Therefore be imitators of God as dear children.
> And walk in love, as Christ also has loved us and
> given Himself for us, an offering and a sacrifice to
> God for a sweet-smelling aroma."
>
> (Ephesians 5:1-2)

Often, we can ask ourselves, how does Jesus want us to become like Him? How do I apply the basics of love as the apostle Paul taught in the Bible? There are many ways He wants us to be conformed into His image, but the number one place to start is to have good soil, a heart of love. We need to let our hearts be opened to His ways first, His truths, so the Word of God can be planted on good soil.

We see with nature how good soil is so essential to creating the right environment for the long-term growth of newly planted seeds so they can germinate and become substantial (see Matthew 13:8). The Bible talks about being doers of the Word, not just hearers (see James 1:22-25).

The Bible is clear we are to let the Word of God be the seed that teaches us Jesus's ways. If we are lifelong students of the Bible, we will have renewed our minds. Sometimes it just takes a short, simple verse in the Bible for the Holy Spirit to plant seeds of grace in our hearts that can last for a lifetime.

Let's start with a powerful seed we can plant right now into our hearts! Romans 12:14 says, "Bless those who persecute you; bless and do not curse." We don't need to memorise the verse numbers for this application for love to come out in our daily actions. We can take in the Word of God and that can be implanted into our hearts, supernaturally empowering us to walk as Jesus did. That is how God wants us to react, so His Word can be richly stored and become germinated seeds of love in our hearts that will bring forth fruit.

Bless and do not curse, yes, even those who hate you! Now that is a characteristic of Jesus. What did Jesus say after He was beaten by the guards who mocked Him, gambled over His belongings, ripped out His beard, and nailed Him to the cross while He slowly suffocated?

> "Then Jesus said, 'Father, forgive them,
> for they do not know what they do.'"
>
> (Luke 23-34)

It is powerful to see Jesus Christ's character of love while He was in agony. He had been sleep-deprived for days before going through this torture, and to have the mind of love toward people still blows my mind.

He prayed those words of grace to the Father, forgive them. He pleaded for their innocence of their actions because they did not believe He was the Son of God and the King of Kings. The self-control and love He has is amazing, and if Jesus can do that while suffering one of the worst executions known, can we not try to love our countrymen over civil issues?

God's word is given to us by the Holy Spirit. As we read His words of life, He enables us with His power to go from having a stony heart of deceit to a heart of flesh with compassion. This is the supernatural power of the Holy Spirit alone; this is His workmanship. But I'll cover more of these aspects soon!

This is all God's design that we are to become love. It is His ultimate plan that has been kept secret from the beginning of time. We are His treasures grafted into the vine, first the Israelites and then the gentiles (see Romans 1:16).

"The mystery which has been hidden from ages and from generations, but now has been revealed to His saints. To them God willed to make known what are the riches of the glory of this mystery among the Gentiles: which is Christ in you, the hope of glory. Him we preach, warning every man and teaching every man in all wisdom, that we may present every man perfect in Christ Jesus."

(Colossians 1:26-28)

Now if you haven't guessed what the mystery is, it is Jesus Christ, the mystery revealed! He was kept from us until the cross; salvation has come not only to the Jews, but to the whole world to be as one family of agape. Agape is a word in Greek that illustrates the greatest form of love, a selfless love for one another. This is what all the prophets of old were prophesying about. Little glimpses of references to Jesus are everywhere in the Tanakh (the Hebrew Bible). For example, Isaiah 53 is revealing Jesus on the cross. It has all been interconnected with a mighty reveal of the suffering Messiah first, before the reigning Messiah returns in triumph for those who are in His spiritual seed through faith! We have His riches of glory dwelling in us with a new heart and His law of love written on our hearts (see Jeremiah 31:33).

> "*Attaining* to all riches of the full assurance of understanding, to the knowledge of the mystery of God, both of the Father and of Christ, in whom are hidden all the treasures of wisdom and knowledge."
>
> (Colossians 2:2-3)

CHAPTER 4

Walk In Love

As mentioned earlier, Ephesians 2:10 says that we should walk in good works, meaning walk in righteousness and love toward others, sharing the good news of hope that is an applied manner of living out our faith. Only the seed of God can bring forth this fruit. A willingness, a love of doing the right thing comes from God working in us.

Do you see how much God loves us? He wants us to be conformed into His image! It's a privilege to be anything like God. Satan fell from his place of authority because of the sin that was found in his heart and he was kicked out of heaven's abode for wanting to be like God. Yet God has given us that privilege. He wants us to be messengers that send the good news to share God's grace and love and to walk in authority just as Jesus walked. Walking means to be in agreement with God's will for our lives.

Jesus sees the bigger picture. He knows that if all His believers are willing to do this, the message of love and the momentum will allow God to use us as His instruments of righteousness with His power in holiness. He desires us to be an alive and zealous church at the end of the age that is His spotless Bride who He is revealing through salvations and obedience to the faith.

"That He might present her to Himself a glorious church, not having spot or wrinkle or any such thing, but that she should be holy and without blemish."

(Ephesians 5:27)

His church is to be in the likeness of Christ. After all, we are called the Body of Christ. If the church is the body of Christ, then is not the head Jesus? The church must understand that we must abide in His love if we are in Christ, so how do we abide? The apostles Peter and John talked about a holy lifestyle of love and discipleship.

"'Be holy for I am holy.'"

(1 Peter 1:16)

"'If you abide in Me, and My words abide in you, you will ask what you desire, and it shall be done for you.'"

(John 15:7)

"'As the Father loved Me, I also have loved you; abide in My love. If you keep My commandments, you will abide in My love, just as I have kept My Father's commandments and abide in His love.'"

(John 15:9-10)

Abiding is being in the Word of God and walking out the faith daily. To obey Jesus is to follow Him. He has commanded us to walk in His love and His characteristics, to live a holy life for the edification of the Body, His church.

Edification is not generally used in modern-day terminology. But at its fundamental basics, it is simply to improve, and that is precisely what the Holy Spirit does in our lives to strengthen us, equip us, and refine us into Christ's image. It's not so much us improving ourselves by our good works. Rather, it's us being willing to let the master craftsman, Jesus, change us in our spiritual man to be reborn and made alive with His power and to transform our core from sin and darkness to light and love. Naturally, we will be changed in our minds, leading to actions that show living and genuine faith. Look at what Jesus was saying to His disciples about how fruit trees can only bear the same kind of fruit that they have been designed and purposed to create. Good fruit starts with the seed and the roots, and the human heart is the origin of good or bad fruit in us. Jesus always likes to use analogies to paint vivid images in His listeners' minds so we can quickly remember His teachings with simplicity.

> "'Every good tree bears good fruit, but a bad tree bears bad fruit. A good tree cannot bear bad fruit, nor *can* a bad tree bear good fruit.'"
>
> (Matthew 7:17-18)

> "'A good man out of the good treasure of his heart brings forth good; and an evil man out of the evil treasure of his heart brings forth evil. For out of the abundance of the heart his mouth speaks.'"
>
> (Luke 6:45)

Jesus is using this analogy for the heart of man. He understood that what comes out of a man's heart is either good or bad depending on the condition of a person's disposition, or "heart" as He explained in Luke. That is why Jesus had to come and give us a new heart of flesh so He can renew our spirit with His empowerment and holiness.

> "Create in me a clean heart, O God,
> And renew a steadfast spirit within me."
>
> (Psalm 51:10)

Jesus loves to teach us from nature about how growth often happens and how it's a journey of learning to walk and become mature in His identity that He gives us. Just like a fruit tree produces fruit in its seasons, the Father is often referred to as a gardener (see John 15:1). He can shape and mould us from His Word and relationship with Him. He can reveal fruits as analogies for us to become abundant with life-giving seeds and to be pleasing to Him by learning of His biblical ways.

We are organic by design, made from dirt, yet immortal in our spirit-man. We are wonderfully and uniquely made (see Psalm 139:14). We are all unique. Jesus has ordained a plan for us to be named in honour and love by the Father. But you may say to me, "Joel, who am I? What can I do?"

It's not who you are. It's who Jesus is and what He can do in your life in a personal and intimate relationship. He knows how everything fits together like a fine ticking watch that is made to perfection. He knows where you are in your life and He knows how to produce His personality in you, if you are willing to become His disciple.

Jesus came to change lives, give hope, encourage us, and bring in harmony so we can be rooted deeply in love like Him. We see that the gospel is for everyone who is willing to listen to Him. It's for those who are broken of heart and are captive in this world. Jesus is the truth bearer that reveals spiritual truths and takes off the blindfolds of the devil. He heals us and gives liberty to all who are under bondage. This is His grace that He gives, and mercy follows when we look to Him as our Saviour.

"'The Spirit of the LORD *is* upon Me,
Because He has anointed Me
To preach the gospel to *the* poor;
He has sent Me to heal the brokenhearted,
To proclaim liberty to *the* captives
And recovery of sight to *the* blind,
To set at liberty those who are oppressed;
To proclaim the acceptable year of the LORD.'"

(Luke 4:18-19)

He can change the way we see our surroundings so we can be the fruit bearer He wants us to be to share this good news to others and help Christ direct paths to eternal salvation. If we know who He is by understanding the Bible and His ways, we will be able to learn to trust Him and to see more of His personality being cultivated in our lives. We too have the Spirit of the Lord in our lives if we believe, and where the Spirit of the Lord is, there is liberty (see 2 Corinthians 3:17-18).

Did you know He wants to be our best friend? Have you ever spent so much time with someone that you start to behave like them? The people we associate with can often bring us either higher or lower. If we spend time in Jesus's presence, if we meditate on the words He teaches, we will surely learn to love and understand Him on a personal level we never thought we could have known.

This is God, the creator of everything, who allows us to be His best friend. He's the one who can help and teach us every day. That is called renewing our hearts and minds to build the character He wants us to have. The best way to know Jesus more is to know His Word. It may seem obvious, but no book can ever compete with the living words Jesus has given to us through the Bible. It is the best-selling book in history for a reason. It has sold more than five billion copies and is increasing each day! [2]

> "That He would grant you … to be strengthened with
> might through His Spirit in the inner man, that Christ
> may dwell in your hearts through faith; that you,
> being rooted and grounded in love may be able …
> to know the love of Christ."
> (Ephesians 3:16-19)

That's precisely what the Bible does: it helps our relationship with Jesus grow. His Holy Spirit can communicate with us to give us strength in this life and help

---

[2] Guiness World Records. "Best-selling book." 2021. https://www.guinnessworldrecords.com/world-records/best-selling-book-of-non-fiction. (Aug. 8, 2022).

increase our roots profoundly. When storms come, we can be grounded in the faith by His power that lives inside our hearts.

Again, we can look at nature and how God has designed the root systems of a tree. The roots are there to support the tree, so nutrition is easily absorbed. The nutrients can help the tree grow healthy. If the roots are not happy or lack moisture, which is the delivery system of the life-giving nutrients, the tree can wither away.

God wants His children to be filled with spiritual nutrients. That comes by hearing the Word of God (see Romans 10:17). Jesus does not want superficial Christians who say they are Christians but do not know Him personally and do not understand His Word. We can't expect to grow if we don't start with the basics of what He has revealed to us in His Word.

His Word is to be our anchor in this life so the Holy Spirit can sow the seeds that will germinate. When we allow the Holy Spirit to give us nutrition, that will correct and direct us. Knowing His ways through the Bible is our steppingstone to a fruitful relationship with hearing His voice. To learn to be like Him requires us to be willing to follow Him and listen to His words. First, we can learn to walk in the ways of Christ, then we can run our race by being obedient to the faith (see Romans 1:5). Discipleship is to be learning of Jesus, which will produce authentic faith to be like Christ (see James 2:14-26 and 2 Timothy 4:7). That is the transformation done by the Holy Spirit in believers' lives as we are willing to allow Him to rule in love and use us as His instrument of righteousness (see Romans 6:13).

CHAPTER 5

Walking in the Spirit

The fruit of the Holy Spirit is a well-known Scripture (see Galatians 5:22-23), and it is an interesting one to look at. In many ways, it shows Jesus's preferred way of life for us and Himself. It can reveal to us who Jesus is and how all His characteristics of love have been shared with us. The Christian walk is about being in His likeness and the sanctification work of the Holy Spirit in our lives, which results in the fruit of the Spirit. It's an applied manner of living from the biblical instructions from the Holy Spirit for a sincere faith.

As we have covered so far about fruits and holiness, you may be thinking there are a lot of good works that have been mentioned to be called a Christian. I am not advocating works-based salvation, rather an authentic faith that has been given to us by grace. It's a gift not earned. Grace is given to us to be our saviour by Jesus Christ. The Bible talks about how we are saved by grace, not of works. Let's cover the verses before Ephesians 2:10 again for a fuller context of the Scriptures.

"For by **grace** you have been **saved through faith**, and that not of yourselves; *it is* **the gift of God**, not of works, lest anyone should boast. For we are His workmanship, created in **Christ Jesus for good works**, which **God prepared beforehand that we should walk in them.**"

(Ephesians 2:8-10, emphasis added)

The Holy Spirit teaches us that we are saved by grace. The pressure is not on us. It's sealed by His grace through our belief and trust in what Jesus did for us on the cross. The Holy Spirit desires us to be willing to allow Him to change us and develop Christ-like identity as a result of receiving grace.

When we have experienced His grace, we are given a helper, the Holy Spirit, who makes us a new creation, when we first believe. A new heart will create new desires. Since we have His Holy Spirit, He allows us to live a life of trust in Him. Jesus wants His disciples to be empowered by the inner working of His Spirit. That's where our journey starts as believers to be more like our king each day, to walk in the Spirit of God and to be in tune with His Son. This is His will is for us: to be nourished by the Holy Spirit, so our lives can become changed indelibly for the better. To receive the full blessings that come along with obedience to the faith is to live and abide in His love. As we draw near to Him, He will draw near to us (see James 4:8).

"But the fruit of the Spirit is love, joy, peace, longsuffering, kindness, goodness, faithfulness, gentleness, self-control. Against such there is no law. And those *who are* Christ's have crucified the flesh with its passions and desires. If we live in the Spirit, let us also walk in the Spirit."

(Galatians 5:22-25)

Galatians teaches us that we should crucify the flesh, which means to apply all aspects that lead to godliness. Godliness is a great gain in spiritual growth. The best way Jesus promotes love and peace in this world is by first changing His creation to become peace bearers who love to do good to fulfil the will of God on earth.

"Righteousness exalts a nation."

(Proverbs 14:34)

Crucifying the flesh—a term that many can struggle to fully comprehend—is to let the Holy Spirit take over our lives. We still live in this world, but we do our best to let the Holy Spirit take over our actions and our lifestyles to change us from within and to listen to the Holy Spirit and His moral judgments. He places knowledge within us of what is acceptable and what is not. We are to release our lives into God's faithful hands and to know that He is going to finish the work that He has started if we stand firm (see Philippians 1:6 and 1 Corinthians 15:2). The saving work is His grace working in our lives and for us to want to follow Jesus, to become His disciples, to become teachable and to have integrity with all the daily actions in life, to be seeking first the kingdom of God and His will. Then we can walk in this new character Jesus has made for us: unique, but also multifaceted like Him. It's us as His masterpiece, a new heart He has given us to be shaped into His character of love, which brings us to the next part: we are a special people.

Do you know God has treasures? Many things are valuable in this life, for example, gold, precious metals, rubies, diamonds, etc, but those things have no eternal value to God. They are as dumb as a wood idol. What value do they have besides their perceived value through scarcity and demand? God is more interested in relationships than He is in material riches. God is a romantic at heart; He loves to Love, and He values relationships as the most precious commodity. He has chosen a people for himself, a nation who was the underdog. This nation was the smallest on earth, but through the Hebrews, God revealed the blessing of abiding in Christ to the entire world.

> "'For you *are* a holy people to the LORD your God; the LORD your God has chosen you to be a people for Himself, a special treasure above all the peoples on the face of the earth. The LORD did not set His love on you nor choose you because you were more in number than any other people, for you were the least of all peoples; but because the LORD loves you.'"
>
> (Deuteronomy 7:6-7)

Through salvation in Christ, we can now inherit the promises and we can become His workmanship and His special treasures. Through belief, we are grafted into the vine of life, the vine of the son of God, Jesus Christ, since we are believing in Him, and we are abiding in love by faith. We were once sinners, now made holy by Jesus and made to be the apple of His eye as well.

God has chosen to bless all the spiritual seed in the faith, and we can be unique treasures to God. It saddens me to think that out of tens of billions of people who have been alive, many have rejected Him and rejected the opportunity to become a valued treasure in the sight of God.

The richness of faith and His promises are available to us because of what God planned for us in His mercy. The detailed lengths He has gone to illustrates a love story of redemption for His people is amazing. It is truly wonderful to see the Bible's rich history of God's actions redeeming us in love. We can see how His people rejected Him, but the unfailing love toward them reveals his lasting new covenant through obedience to Christ and keeping the faith (see 2 Timothy 4:7).

I'm not advocating for a replacement of the Jewish people, but rather a merging of God's grace to all people since He is the God of all creation. His chosen people, the Israelites, will fit perfectly in His branch when they have the veil removed leading to salvation through belief. Let's continue walking in fruitfulness as a result of receiving grace.

Naturally, if we are walking in love, the fruit of the Spirit will follow. We will want to pursue the faith; we will not want to resist the Holy Spirit like the Israelites in the wilderness. Instead, we will want to please Him. We don't want to do the things of the flesh, and we will naturally hate the things of the old man. It's a beautiful work of love done through the resurrection power.

Although it may be painful to lose our life, Jesus says those who lose their lives will find eternal life; this is what He is talking about. As Jesus was lifted on the cross, He was slowly suffocated. It shows us how the Father wants to gradually cut and prune the negative, harmful desires of the flesh out of our lives and bring forth good fruit in His seasons and times. It's to be one with Jesus and to have the mind of Christ. The mind of Christ is not something that is simply unattainable, as some may claim. It is a simple attitude of trust and obedience to apply the words of His teachings into our hearts, to have access and a rapport with who Jesus is and how He wants us to follow him.

> *"There is* therefore now no condemnation to those
> who are in Christ Jesus, who do not walk according
> to the flesh, but according to the Spirit."
>
> (Romans 8:1)

There's no judgment to those who are in Jesus. Romans 8:1 is telling us that if we are walking in His Spirit, we are not going to be condemned. Walking in the Spirit is to have the mind of Christ. What our minds conceive and think leads to our actions: either good or bad. To allow the Holy Spirit to prune and correct us, it's essential to understand what the fruit of the Spirit are. By doing that, we renew our minds in the Bible. By being diligent in the Bible, we can allow the Spirit to change us and make corrections in our life, big or small, as we walk out our journey in knowing Him. We will grow in the knowledge of grace and Jesus Christ. Sometimes we can think we know the Bible, and sometimes we can say we don't need to read it anymore. That's a mistake: to know the Holy Spirit's fruit is a journey. No one who reads a book once or twice takes it completely in, let alone applies the teachings in their lives. If only we could grow that quick! But God knows we are on a spiritual journey.

The Holy Spirit will do micro-adjustments in your perception of who He is every time you read the Bible. Doing that can instil strength into you and a higher reverence for Jesus. I can go through the Bible, and sometimes I think to myself, "Hmm, what will I learn this time…" To my surprise, after reading or listening, I think, "I'm glad I did. I learned something new again." And that happens every single time! God's Word is manifold, and when we are ready, the Holy Spirit teaches us His revelations and the spiritual food we need to grow in the season we are in.

The Holy Spirit does not expect perfection from us, but to grow in grace and to build a living relationship with Him. People often go to different types of literature to learn revelation from man's understanding, which is a helpful tool, but too often we can become stagnant and rely on others to spoon feed us. By doing so, we are missing the direct source of the wealth and knowledge of Jesus. We need to rely on the Holy Spirit to guide us and correct us by His Word so we can learn of His fruit and be made in His image.

As we covered, Romans 8:1 gives us the knowledge we are no longer condemned if we are living in God's spirit of love, learning, leaning, and seeking Him in our lives. But let's dig a little deeper to exactly what the fruit of the Spirit are and what they are not.

> "I say then: Walk in the Spirit, and you shall not fulfill the lust of the flesh. For the flesh lusts against the Spirit, and the Spirit against the flesh; and these are contrary to one another, so that you do not do the things that you wish. But if you are led by the Spirit, you are not under the law."
>
> (Galatians 5:16-18)

Sometimes people can have a hard time understanding what walking in the Spirit is, and I can understand why. It can be overcomplicated. There are many moving parts and different interpretations of abiding in Christ and seeing fruitfulness brought out in our lives by the Holy Spirit's power. But let's take the text for what it is.

Let's look at not walking in the Spirit. It's contrary to love. Oil and water do not mix. Bad fruit and good fruit cannot be on the same tree, as we talked about. One cannot be the other. Sure, we in this fallen world still live in our fallen nature and we will get angry or sin. But it's important to know we have an advocate, Jesus Christ, who forgives us of our wrongdoings. We don't take grace for granted, but we aim for righteousness and love, to let grace equip us for empowerment for victory over sin and death through faith in Jesus Christ, who holds the key.

"Now the works of the flesh are evident, which are: adultery, fornication, uncleanness, lewdness, idolatry, sorcery, hatred, contentions, jealousies, outbursts of wrath, selfish ambitions, dissensions, heresies, envy, murders, drunkenness, revelries, and the like; of which I tell you beforehand, just as I also told *you* in time past, that those who practice such things will not inherit the kingdom of God."

(Galatians 5:19-21)

We see the consequence is clear if we are practising these things, but what does practising mean? I know we know what practising means, but let's get technical because sometimes we can allow irrational fears try to condemn us.

48

The Oxford Dictionary defines practise as "Carry out or perform (a particular activity, method, or custom) habitually or regularly.
[Ex.] 'We still practise some of these rituals today.'"

If we are always acting in such a manner, that does not show actual signs of a repented heart. The flesh will lust for these things, and the Holy Spirit will empower those who have a repented heart to overcome the fallen nature. He gives us the power as we are willing to let Him. We may commit or have committed one of these sins, but it does not mean we regularly practice them. If we are born again, we will hate the sin that our flesh tries to lust after, and we will agree with the Holy Spirit that it is evil. Just as the Apostle Paul states:

> "For what I am doing, I do not understand. For what
> I will to do, that I do not practice; but what I hate, that I do.
> If then, I do what I will not to do, I agree with the law
> that *it is* good. But now, *it is* no longer I who do it,
> but sin that dwells in me."
>
> (Romans 7:15-17)

Sin can influence us and try to get our flesh to walk in its carnal ways, and that is sin that dwells in us. But we do not live according to those desires, but according to the Holy Spirit's power and the law of love.

We may get angry or be jealous, or do many other things listed there. But we have the grace of God to forgive us and transform us to walk in the Holy Spirit's power of love. By being in the Bible and knowing what is right and what is not, we can become vessels of honour to the Lord and become the treasures of holiness that He desires His people to be. Let's look now at the flipside of the flesh, the liberty of love.

Jesus said if we love, it will fulfil the law. Jesus obeyed His Father's commandments, and now we have a new commandment to love one another as He loved us. Under the Holy Spirit's inspiration, the apostle Paul is letting us know how to walk out our Christian journey with love.

"But the fruit of the Spirit is love, joy, peace, longsuffering, kindness, goodness, faithfulness, gentleness, self-control. Against such there is no law. And those *who are* Christ's have crucified the flesh with its passions and desires. If we live in the Spirit, let us also walk in the Spirit. Let us not become conceited, provoking one another, envying one another."
(Galatians 5:22-26)

The fruit of the spirit is the work of the Holy Spirit; that's why it's called His fruit! But we need to be willing to put to death the passions and desires that produce rotten fruit (the flesh) and then we can be changed to grow into His loving characteristics. We can gain His knowledge of what is correct, and our hearts can now be changed supernaturally by His grace. The result of good fruit will be given to us by our willingness to accept His ways.

I was preparing for a sermon one week, and I discovered some effective Bible verses relating to blessing others. Jesus wants us to all walk in the fruit of love, patience, and long-suffering. One verse that is powerful I believe resonates with Jesus' character, and it revealed to me the latitude of His love. Since preparing for that sermon allowed the depth of His understanding into my heart, although not perfected ... but it resonates to my response with the power of Christ within. As I briefly covered before about blessing those who come against you, let's have a look at how Jesus can give us His power to retain these sayings in our hearts, so we can apply the Word of God in our daily walk.

> "Bless those who persecute you;
> bless and do not curse."
>
> (Romans 12:14)

It's wonderful how the Holy Spirit can remind us of these words of wisdom given to us by Jesus and He brings them to our remembrance for us to take note of in moments when we may need them. I was on my local street waiting in line to go to the shop. While waiting, a man approached me, swearing and judging me for things I had not done. I looked around, and to my surprise, yes, he was talking to me. As he approached me, he was violently looking for war. I patiently responded to his abuse and said, in a kind manner, "No, I do not think I'm better than you," and then let him continue with threats against my safety. The Holy Spirit gave me the empowerment to stand there and keep silent. The man then spat in my face and continued walking away. Now, in my flesh, I could have reacted and started a fight after his provoking and personal assaults.

But the fruit of Jesus dismissed his abuse, and my ego was put aside to allow humility to defuse the situation. Jesus showed me His way of de-escalating the problem rather than adding fuel to the fire. After that, I thought to myself, "Wow, that person will not go far if he keeps doing that. What a low life." But then I thought he was in a blinded state of anger toward others. He may have had it hard in life and is angry at society. He is on a journey, and at this point, he is lost and hurt.

Instead of cursing him and saying, "Oh God, did you see what he just did to me?", that verse came to mind: "bless and do not curse." That's what the Holy Spirit taught me. Now I could have listened to my carnal nature and made problems worse, but instead, I let the Holy Spirit's fruit come out. I prayed that he might come to know the love of God and repent for his bad fruit and turn to know Jesus, who brings the best out of all of us.

Here's how the fruit was shown in that situation: Christ's **love** was to pray for him after I was threatened. **Peace** brought forth from the Holy Spirit, who did not start a fight. **Longsuffering** was the wisdom to not fight back with anger. **Goodness, kindness,** and **gentleness** were to keep calm and show care. **Faithfulness** was to listen to Jesus Christ's ways, and **self-control** was not to punch him in the face!

That's Jesus and His Spirit. If I had not had the knowledge of Christ and His attributes, how could the Holy Spirit bring those understandings to remembrance? For me to bless that man and ask for His salvation is a better way, rather than for him to stay lost in his ways and be condemned. Love is the key to opening hearts and changing people within.

When Jesus was on His way to Jerusalem, as told in Luke 9, He was looking for a place to stay. He sent word by messenger to Samaritans to find a place to stay overnight, but this town rejected Him because Jesus was not staying there very long. His disciples had recently been arguing about who was to be greater in the kingdom of heaven (Luke 9:46-48).

John and James asked if they should call fire out of heaven to judge the town, referring to Elijah and how he called fire out of the sky to burn the false prophets. The Samaritans were half Jewish and had mixed with other surrounding beliefs. They rejected blessings of the Messiah coming to stay with them for one night. It was quite possibly an insult to the disciples. They would have been upset that Samaritans would show such disregard to the Anointed One. Jesus could have cursed them, but that's hardly His character to act so quickly and harshly; Jesus understood their unbelief and decided to bless other surrounding villages who were open and welcoming to the gospel of peace that Jesus was sowing.

"And when His disciples James and John saw *this*, they said, 'Lord, do You want us to command fire to come down from heaven and consume them, just as Elijah did?'

But He turned and rebuked them, and said, 'You do not know what manner of spirit you are of. For the Son of Man did not come to destroy men's lives but to save *them*.'"

(Luke 9:54-56)

We see Jesus rebuked James and John. He said they were not acting in the Spirit of Love. Elijah had the correct judgment toward the wickedness of the false prophets' actions and the spirit of Jezebel. But the disciples were thinking according to pride and not discerning love and righteousness. Jesus stated that He doesn't want to destroy people's lives, but rather to show them love and save them!

It's essential to see Jesus's perspective of love and to understand how He sees who we are in Him, and how He values our eternal souls. He sees us as His children; we are His heirs to the throne. We are adopted into His family of grace and given titles and positions in heavenly places. It's not His judgment that blesses us, rather it's His mercy that is longsuffering that reveals to us opportunities of salvation. We are rich in God's mercy for the kingdom's blessings.

"Making mention of you in my prayers: that ... the eyes of your understanding being enlightened; that you may know what is the hope of His calling, what are the riches of the glory of His inheritance in the saints, and what *is* the exceeding greatness of His power toward us who believe."
(Ephesians 1:16-19)

Through belief, we are rich, but the Samaritans declined to host Christ's short stay and they rejected a blessing from God. It would have been a new light for the town to see His compassion and wisdom, not to mention the healing miracles Jesus would have performed over the short span that He would have been led to stay with them, although He did bless the Samaritans through a woman's testimony at the well that revealed He had come for sinners and to give mercy to those who are lost but have a believing heart.

It's a lesson in knowing Jesus. He blesses us through belief and acceptance of Him. He was sent by the Father's will to that town but was rejected out of unbelief and jealousy. By belief, we are blessed and seated in the heavens with Him in this age of grace, yet the world can be like a type of Samaria: unwilling and unbelieving toward Jesus, and they can forfeit blessings. To be walking in the Spirit is to be in belief to God's ways and to be open to His invitations and not fulfilling the fleshly desires that can include jealousy like the Samaritans had, but rather let the Holy Spirit be welcomed in. In the next chapter, I will cover how abiding in God's vine is not just physical, but rather spiritual and what the works of the flesh are and how it is contradictory to walking in the Spirit.

CHAPTER 6
Abiding in God's Family Fruit Vine

God's family is vast. There are natural offspring from Abraham. Many can come from Jewish decent with the diaspora of the Israel's people. The word diaspora is a translation of a Greek word that means to "sow over." [3] They were scattered amongst other nations, although Israel had experienced diaspora before through the judgments of God because of their severe disobedience. At the time of Jesus's ministry, scholars have suggested there were most likely already more Jewish people living abroad than in Israel at the time. Research indicates that after the Roman Empire scattered the Hebrews in A.D. 70, they went to all parts of the world and helped form some major civilizations and blended in over generations. [4] Many adapted to different cultures and beliefs without fully understanding their history or origin. As many as the sands of the sea are the children of Abraham:

[3] Britannica, T. Editors of Encyclopaedia. "diaspora." *Encyclopedia Britannica*, May 23, 2014. https://www.britannica.com/topic/diaspora-social-science. (Aug. 8, 2022)

[4] Richard Hooker. "Ancient Jewish History-The Diaspora." Jewish Virtual Library. n.d. https://www.jewishvirtuallibrary.org/the-diaspora (Aug. 8, 2022)

"Therefore from one man, and him as good as dead, were born *as many* as the stars of the sky in multitude—innumerable as the sand which is by the seashore."

(Hebrews 11:12)

"'I will multiply your descendants as the stars of the heaven and as the sand which *is* on the seashore; and your descendants shall possess the gate of their enemies. In your seed all the nations of the earth shall be blessed, because you have obeyed My voice.'"

(Genesis 22:17-19)

Scripture reveals the extent of the promise given to Abraham and his descendants. There are many Israelites all around the world that have come from the physical seed of Abraham, and most likely do not know their true linage due to the diaspora! But Jesus wants to bring everyone into the spiritual seed of Abraham, which is belief and faith in God. Romans 2:28–29 states to be a Jew is from the heart not the outward appearance of the flesh, but rather from the Spirit of God. Romans later reveals that God seals us as His sons and daughters as we are now adopted in and "Abba," meaning father, is our God (see Romans 8:15). Being from the physical seed of Abraham does not have eternal saving power as some religious leaders thought, but there were faithful promises given to Abraham that God would prosper his physical descendants as well as His spiritual ones, and Jesus will be faithful to make them a part of God's spiritual vine that leads to salvation through the royal sacrifice of the Messiah. You will find out more about it later when we cover more details about the second coming and the bride being fully revealed with one of the greatest love stories in progress!

We were once sons of disobedience, according to Ephesians 2. The chapter talks about how we all once conducted ourselves in the sinful natures of lust and fulfilling the fleshly desires that lead to rotten fruit. Regardless of who we are or where we come from, Jesus's plan is redemption for the world. Let's have another look at the fruit of the Spirit in that Bible passage to reiterate the human condition and the love of God.

"And you *He made alive*, who were dead in trespasses and sins, in which you once walked according to the course of this world, according to the prince of the power of the air, the spirit who now works in the sons of disobedience, among whom also we all once conducted ourselves in the lusts of our flesh, fulfilling the desires of the flesh and of the **mind**, and were by **nature** children of **wrath, just as the others.**

"But God, who is rich in mercy, because of His great love with which He loved us, even when we were dead in trespasses, made us alive together with Christ (by grace you have been saved), and raised *us* up together, and made *us* sit together in the heavenly *places* in Christ Jesus, that in the ages to come He might show the exceeding riches of His grace in *His* kindness toward us in Christ Jesus." (Ephesians 2:1-7, emphasis added)

Once again, the Bible teaches us the fruit of the Spirit and what it is not; in this fallen world, the prince of the power controls this world through those who lust after sinful desires. They are entrapped to him as a "ruler" through their disobedience. We were in the past sinners who were controlled by the flesh's rebellious nature. It's essential to remember the human fallen nature is not the natural desires God made us with, but the corrupted nature we inherited from our actions and agreement to partake in sin.

Jesus came to give us His goodness and the attributes of love by His inner working and power. Notice how the apostle Paul talks about the mind is where sin starts and can germinate. He gives us an understanding that what we allow to be planted in our minds—either good or bad—can result in sin or righteousness.

That doesn't mean because we may have sinful ideas that they will result in bearing bad fruit. Rather, it's the indulgence of the mind and lust that can attract us more than the ideas that can lead to sin.

If we meditate on God's Word, our minds will be more on the Spirit of God and allow the germination of holiness and the fruit can be more prominent in our lives. This verse exhibits God's mercy, love, and goodwill toward us, who were children of wrath. Wrath is a straightforward and direct approach to the fallen nature of mankind. We were indeed wrath. Who wants to be wrathful and to live in wrath? It's tiring and full of mess.

We see many people who have lived successful lives but become addicted to different activities that can lead to immediate danger and wrath. No amount of success will ever take away our nature of wrath and pain. It's Christ who replaces wrath with His life-giving Spirit unto peace.

That peace is an aspect we so eagerly want for ourselves, but through many fallen attempts, or through false religions or man's efforts, true inner contentment will never be achieved. "Why?" you may ask. Simply put, it's impossible. Without Jesus, it is vanity. We cannot put to death our fallen human nature without the Holy Spirit's empowerment to fill the void of what is full of wrath.

There have been many attempts to change the human mind and its sinful ways. Some religions try meditating, others try a form of starvation from pleasures, and others use pain to humble themselves. To try and change sinful nature with man's efforts is futile and is only possible through the majestic creator who holds the key. Many religions leave it to man, and it's about how good we are or what we've done: it all relies on our efforts. It's pride to say, "This is what I have done." Humility says, "This is what love has done!"

The Bible talks about how we are to be filled with the Spirit. A few terms can relate to different meanings of being filled, but to be filled is to allow the Holy Spirit to take up complete residence and create that new character moulded into the image of Jesus Christ. To be filled is to be overflowing into other people's lives. It will show the fruit of the Spirit if we learn of the Holy Spirit and let Him do it rather than our attempts from our religions. By resting in God's love, we will have His peace and joy in our lives in all situations and find rest in Jesus's arms. When we are at rest within ourselves, then we will be able to show stability to others around us.

Have you ever walked into a room with someone who is in a bad mood? I know I have, and I've probably done the same to others also. It can change the other person's perspective, and they can become adapted to your frustrations or vice versa. It takes a resilient person not to be changed negatively by others around them who act in such a way. Well, the fruit of the Spirit first come from Jesus, and when we walk in His peaceful ways, we can enter a room with happiness and cheer others up when they are down. Likewise, positivity and love can change people's perspective and give hope.

Fellowship with other Christians can bring us up and allow the love of God to be contagious in a good way! Jesus can influence us for the positive to become fruitful. We can be empowered by Jesus; likewise His followers will bring forth fruitfulness of His love too! Being Christians in this world, we must have that mindset to be fruitful. We need to set the room's atmosphere to change the mood. If we are joyful because of Jesus, we must let that flow out of us, be resilient from the negativity, and understand that greater is the one who lives in me than the one who lives in the world. Let the Spirit overflow out of us and change that room; become the salt and light within a place that can be often dark.

> "Do not be overcome by evil,
> but overcome evil with good."
>
> (Romans 12:21)

People in the fallen world who have not come to the knowledge of Jesus Christ are children of wrath by default like we were once. They are seeking the fleshly lust to fulfil because they do not know Christ. We as Christians can be fruitful by sharing the good news and sowing seeds. By doing all things in love, we will open hearts and allow germination of the gospel of peace.

Many Christians pray to God, "Just take me over." It doesn't work that way, and to pray such a prayer is not practical. God did not create us to be robots with no will so we could be taken over. He wants us to lay our desires down and obey Him in love. By doing so, we are a team with God and He will allow us to grow in, by yielding to His will and allowing Jesus to move through us. He will not violate our will. We can pray for empowerment as we look to Jesus and what He would do in all situations. When we walk by faith and learn to lean on Jesus, He can start the transformative work by His Holy Spirit and the washing of the Word to make that new man complete in all good works. In a process of sanctification, we will progress from old self and wrathful nature to love inspired by God. Jesus does equal love when we allow Him to take us over.

As Paul said in Ephesians 2, we are heirs to His riches of grace and he prayed that we will know the exceeding riches that He has prepared for us. We have been seated in a place of authority because of what Jesus has done for us. With authority comes responsibility, and to be living in His Spirit is the start of such riches.

Do you know even the angels investigate the riches that we have received: that God Himself died for us while we are in our nature of wrath? Now by grace, we enter into His nature of love. Here is a Bible passage that teaches us to be clothed with love. We find unity comes with having Christ's heart, which is walking in the Spirit, letting Christ rule in us.

"Since God chose you to be the holy people he loves, you must clothe yourselves with tenderhearted mercy, kindness, humility, gentleness, and patience. Make allowance for each other's faults, and forgive anyone who offends you. Remember, the Lord forgave you, so you must forgive others. Above all, clothe yourselves with love, which binds us all together in perfect harmony. And let the peace that comes from Christ rule in your hearts. For as members of one body you are called to live in peace. And always be thankful.

> "Let the message about Christ,
> in all its richness, fill your lives."
>
> (Colossians 3:12-16 NLT)

CHAPTER 7

Treasures of Heaven and Our Spiritual Mind

To be transformed into His image is a privilege, and it is our spiritual right as believers to be given His qualities, which He releases through His Holy Spirit, permeating like a sweet fragrance into our lives. He reveals the unique treasures of His heart to us so we can learn of His creativity, which produces renewed minds.

In the gospels, Jesus always reminds His disciples about the rewards given to those who serve Him. As if His love is not enough, He crowns us with eternal life that provides a way for us to get out of the snares of sin. He has also chosen to declare us royalty as vessels of honour and make us treasures worth the blood of Christ. That is the value He has put on us. It's not that we were ever valuable within ourselves (see Proverbs 6:12 and Isaiah 64:6), but His choice to sacrifice to save us makes us valuable and we belong to the Father (see 1 Corinthians 6:20).

Jesus wants us to have a renewed approach to the correct eternal values, and when we are seeking His truths, we will have changed hearts, and that gives us the treasures of heaven. In return, we will be pleasing to the Lord and be precious to Him. Let's have a look at what Jesus taught His disciples about seeking treasures and where our hearts are focused.

"'Do not lay up for yourselves treasures on earth,
where moth and rust destroy and where thieves break in
and steal; but lay up for yourselves treasures in heaven,
where neither moth nor rust destroys and where
thieves do not break in and steal. For where your
treasure is, there your heart will be also.'"

(Matthew 6:19–21)

Jesus is teaching a manifold truth here. God's Word can have a large number of lessons in each passage. Each verse that Jesus teaches has eternal impact on the believer's mind. First, He says to not lay up for yourself goods on this earth. They will soon fade away and become worthless by decay and age, or thieves will steal our goods in this unsecure world. Family lines and heritages dwindle and are often taken away by others who rise in place of the past forgotten glories.

He continues to share a deeper reality of the matter: God's kingdom is where treasure will be secure and what is rightly yours will be given to you and kept safe. Where our hearts lay will be where the treasure is, whether it is of value or not. If your heart is set on the world and the short passing pleasures, you will want to store up for yourself valuables here. But it will ultimately lead to becoming worthless since we are in a decaying world.

But if your heart is for God, you will see clearly to be storing up wealth in heaven. It will be a grander retirement package where righteousness hands out just rewards. Jesus teaches that if we lose family because of the gospel or we lose valuable goods and desirable things, He will return them to us one hundredfold in eternal life if we seek His kingdom first and if we are last because of us serving Him for His name. Those rewards will never be taken away by death, thieves, or the decay of time (see Mark 10:29-30).

In the parable of the unjust steward in Luke 16, Jesus told a story about how the master of the house heard a bad report of his servant wasting his goods. The steward was given a short time to finish his business dealings and inform the different people about their debts and how much they owed.

Jesus says that while this unjust steward had done wrong, he was too prideful to become a beggar, and with his bad report in town, he would certainly never be trusted again with any house's goods. So, he acted swiftly by setting the affairs of the house in order.

The shrewd, unjust steward reduced the bills owing on the accounts so the farmers and business owners would only have to pay back a fraction of the debt. The unjust servant gained favour with the community by releasing them from years of possible debt. He made new friends who could help him after being removed from his duties. The master of the house found out and commended him on his actions because it was clever.

> "'So the master commended the unjust steward because he had dealt shrewdly. For the sons of this world are more shrewd in their generation than the sons of light.'"
>
> (Luke 16:8)

Jesus has a few teachings within this parable, but one of them is this: if the world knew and believed of the eternal kingdom that is full of abundance, wealth, and blessings that

God gives to His children, how well advertised would the gospel be preached for fruitfulness? How shrewd would the sons of this world be in seeking the kingdom of God if they believed the reality of heaven and the rewards Jesus teaches about?

Jesus was not promoting doing wrong, but this is one of the few parables that does not talk about any righteous act or Jesus's or the Father's direct will, but a bit of wisdom in being bright for gain. Jesus may have had a group of listeners who were some disciples who were willing to do good while others were Pharisees who were wicked with the wealth that they had acquired.

God wants His people to be wise with their money and use their talents to progress the gospel and save souls, make friends, and share the eternal home with others. We can use our riches in this life to invest it for God's plans and purposes. Doing the will of God can increase our wealth one hundredfold if we want to sincerely give toward the gospel's goal: to save souls.

That does not mean you are to give all your money away or be careless with life's opportunities, but we are to be wise and to use our time and money as a tool to promote the gospel, to support ministers and communities, and to build better prospects for the gospel to be shared.

If we look at some past wealthy business entrepreneurs, they would often be shrewd in their dealings to acquire business to build their kingdom. Often some wealthy business entrepreneurs took over news outlets to print their stories that created an ebb and flow of opportunities that changed some modern-day paradigms. William Randolph Hearst believed he was not reporting history but instead making it. We see Hearst's history as one of the first business tycoons who helped shape America's history and developed the news industry as we know it today. [5]He was a shrewd businessman who took his beliefs into changing the way the America people saw their country, and his outlets were compared to the presidential influence over the country. He was a pioneer for many others who followed after him in the news industry. Hearst understood the incredible influence news has over the way people perceive facts and beliefs. I'm not saying that to manipulate the population is a good thing, but what I am sharing is that as Christians, we are to be Christ's ambassadors to change the way people see Jesus, so we can share God's love to people. If Christians can have influential people in places of reach to help shape the world for Christ's ways, we as Christians should aspire to be as shrewd for Christ's kingdom as we can to reach more and to help bring repentance to a land so God can deal favourably with His people.

> "'If My people who are called by My name will
> humble themselves, and pray and seek My face, and
> turn from their wicked ways, then I will hear from heaven,
> and will forgive their sin and heal their land.'"
>
> (2 Chronicles 7:14)

---

[5] "William Randolph Hearst," PBS *American Experience* video, aired Sept. 27, 2021, https://www.thirteen.org/programs/american-experience/william-randolph-hearst/

We are in the business of news, the good news! Not that it's our motive to store up money, rather it's to invest into God's will to reach more people and to be united as one in Christ's family. After all, Jesus said the harvest is ripe, but the labourers are few.

Souls are ready to be harvested (see Matthew 9:35-38). Many people are interested in returns of money, rather than exchanging money for advertisement of the gospel. How valuable is one human soul? These are the questions we need to ask ourselves: what is the worth of a soul saved from eternal judgement? We can choose our own fate, but if exposed to the gospel by any means necessary, we can be directed and changed by His love.

A paid billboard sharing a short message of the hope that Christ gives could reach someone before they attempt to commit suicide. How much money is a human soul worth to us? It's priceless. It cannot be bought by our money, but we can use our money as a tool to share that Jesus overcame this world to set us free. Is one dollar too much to share the good news? Now I'm not saying we need money to advance the gospel, but it's an extra tool that can be used to convert it for fruitfulness! We want to be a church that is associated with charity and love rather than asking for money.

If Christian leaders and the body of Christ work in unity (see Acts 2:44-46), we can achieve a better balance to help be well assisted and have more productivity within the natural means of advancing the gospel to let people know who Christ is and what hope He gives us! We see Jesus and the twelve apostles changed the world with the power of the Holy Spirit alone, so we see that it's by the power of the Holy Spirit and being led to ignite movement that can spark a generational revival on fire for God. Although there is more complexly to the world and new ways to reach people with technology and advancements, God wants us to use all means to gain God's kingdom and to reach souls.

On a large-scale Jesus and the church does not want to be associated with money, but rather love. We all need to use money daily, but to be seeking money first can cause significant problems in one's life (see 1 Timothy 6:17, 1 Timothy 6:9-10, Matthew 19:16-22, Matthew 6:24, Matthew 6:33, and Acts 8:20). Too many churches can preach money and a life full of prosperity and worldly gain over the kingdom's gain and the true eternal riches. There can be perverted gospels that share half-truths (see Galatians 1:8) rather than the love of Christ and salvation being shared. The gospel can be used for worldly gain, but it shouldn't be so by church leaders.

Christians are largely not being taught to pick up their cross daily and follow Christ with all they have (see Luke 9:23). We see that Scripture shares the opposite of the majority of prosperity taught to some groups. The true gospel is often described as through trials and tribulations that we can face in this world, and we are rewarded for our faithfulness toward God's kingdom so we enter rejoicing (see Acts 14:22 and Matthew 5:10-11). But in saying this, it's not all one size fits all; there are plans and purposes of God that change the way Christians can pursue God and have an honest and shrewd godly gain, but the key is godly gain and not our own.

If we are using our resources wisely, we can be shrewd for the kingdom of God. We can progress the gospel at a greater rate than ever before in history because of our society's reach. We can exchange our goods for God's will and give sincerely to the gospel. We may lose family members because they don't understand our choices to help one another in this world when it makes no sense, but Christ has given us a promise and an inheritance. If we lose what we have because of the gospel, it will be returned to us one hundred-fold.

To share the gospel is the most important objective. Content on the internet, for example, can be viewed millions of times from the other side of the world in minutes! The apostle Paul on his journeys had to deal with shipwrecks, toils in the deep, and interactions with robbers on the road. It was hard for him to reach destinations. Sometimes it took months to travel places he needed to go, but times have changed. We can be more innovative in how Jesus can be proclaimed and shared in modern-day society through films, music, athletics, and brands acquiring gospel truths.

A paradigm can be created to see a greater multitude come into the kingdom of heaven. Jesus is the captain at the front, leading the troops. We need to be willing and ready in His will to listen so we can respond to the plans of God. If we allow Him to transform our lives, we will want to seek people being saved, and the treasures of our hearts will make these adjustments to society to share the good news.

We must be competent and serve God with integrity and use the world's money to build the kingdom of heaven in terms of souls won. God wants us to be faithful with the little we have, and if we are steadfast in the little, He can give us more to be reliable with (Luke 16:10). That's not to say it will be easy to do so—there will always be people who try and stop us from sharing the gospel—but with patience and perseverance, it will lead to fruitfulness.

"Do not be deceived, God is not mocked; for whatever a man sows, that he will also reap. For he who sows to his flesh will of the flesh reap corruption, but he who sows to the Spirit will of the Spirit reap everlasting life. And let us not grow weary while doing good, for in due season we shall reap if we do not lose heart. Therefore, as we have opportunity, let us do good to all, especially to those who are of the household of faith."

(Galatians 6:7-10)

Jesus's perspective is so different from man's. He sees the big and small. He weighs the sacrifice from the heart. For example, in Mark 12:41-44, when many people were giving an offering to the temple, many rich people were giving out of their abundance thousands each, but a poor old widow came and gave just two cents. Jesus said that she had given more than everyone else because she gave all that she had.

Jesus sees the intentions, the sacrifices, and the motives within the heart. Who has a greater reward? The widow who gave two cents? Or the Pharisees giving thousands from their abundance? The reason why I am bringing this to your attention is this: God sees the small we do. God will be faithful when it's time to reveal our labours in Christ's love. The judgment seat of Christ and rewards Christians can receive are going to be based on the motives of our heart, not from man's understanding, rather from God's great understanding. The valuable treasure is you and your time, decisions, and commitments to serve Jesus

Christ to share the gospel. Small or big, there will be a just reward. The first will be last, and the last will be first. As an old preacher once said to me, "The person who holds the door open for the congregation who is last may be first in God's kingdom." The lowest tasks done, or the most overlooked jobs, may be rewarded when we have an honest motive to serve just as Jesus also came to serve.

> "'For even the Son of Man came not to be served but to serve others and to give his life as a ransom for many."
>
> (Matthew 20:28 NLT)

Understanding the true riches is to understand we must become love to help others in need, just as Jesus came to serve and to wash the disciples' feet and to lay down His life for His creation. Understanding this reveals Christ's humility to us, so we can renew our perspectives into the mind of Christ and the valuable lessons that the humble can receive to be lowly in mind. To seek first the kingdom of God is to build His kingdom through working together as a body, a unit. By doing so, it can open unlimited possibilities. We may not necessarily see the full scope of our labour in love, but the reality of the spiritual application of first seeking God's kingdom will open up blessings for us as we continue to do so (see Matthew 6:33).

Renewing our minds from the fallen nature is so often done by receiving humility and having a willing and contrite spirit. We need to listen to Jesus's teachings and let the Word of God into our hearts by meditating on His sayings and letting the spiritual application feed our inner man.

It's essential to know that as a body, we can all be building a better eternal home with greater prospects that lead to better rewards than this world could ever offer. Yet very few find this path of life because it is out of this world, and what is out of our sight and minds can easily be forgotten. Many can be unwise in building the kingdom of God because Christians can sometimes be naive and less shrewd for sincere godly gain. Jesus's teachings show us that God rewards sacrifice, love, diligence, and belief. Great gain can be achieved with a renewed mindset of the eternal kingdom that Jesus has prepared for us. His teachings reveal to us the wonderful promises of great return and help us press on toward the upward call of Jesus.

"Christ ... loved the church and gave Himself for her, that He might sanctify and cleanse her with the washing of water by the word, that He might present her to Himself a glorious church."

(Ephesians 5:25-27)

"Do not be conformed to this world, but be transformed by the renewing of your mind, that you may prove what *is* that good and acceptable and perfect will of God."

(Romans 12:2)

The Bible verses above share powerful instructions. The apostle Paul understood about gaining the knowledge of Christ to help our minds be prepared for doing God's will. He shares that the regenerative power of the Holy Spirit is critical to shape our minds to create love in our lives. Paul is giving us in-depth insight into the process of the Holy

Spirit's sanctifying ways. It's the Word of God that cleanses our minds and helps us not be conformed to the carnal ideas or practices in this life.

Let's briefly go over different aspects advertising uses to capture the attention of the mind of people in the modern world. There is power in suggestion that industries use to direct people to conform to brands, and the power of advertising can help people feel relatable, valuable, and identifiable. If we look at how valuable advertising is in this world and the power of suggestion to direct us to different sources, there is real estate for people's attention everywhere, advertisements for fast food, tech, music, movies, and TV series. Look at New York's Times Square, for example. We are living in a world that values real estate that can reach the minds of people to generate loyalty toward businesses.

Space has never been more valuable. People's minds have never been in such a war of influence ever in history. There is such a high price on people's minds; industries understand that it makes money. We live in a fallen world full of greed and indulgent behaviour through lust. The traps have been laid by the gains to be made, and it can lead many away from God and pierce them with many sorrows (see 1 Timothy 6:10).

Real estate is becoming virtual more so now, and with the new world of technologies evolving, it's becoming a part of people's daily activities almost every waking second. We see algorithms suggesting trends and directing people's behaviour and knowledge, which can lead to lustful traps of a false reality created to entertain selfish behaviour, rather than motivate love.

The source of human values is placed upon people's minds and beliefs of society. What gets fed into our minds can have a tremendous impact on what manifests out of our hearts. Our minds show the intentions that can lead to our actions being changed. If we expose our minds to evil, we can become desensitised to evil and fall into sin's snares. The devil can use people's greed and fallen nature to advertise sin as cool or exciting. The fallen nature feeds on this behaviour. But it never reaches lasting refreshment. We will always want bigger and better things to satisfy. He will use any means possible to snare people away from the truth and to take unbelievers' minds or even to draw the saints away from the faith of God. The temptation of the carnal mind enslaves the old man that results in sin.

"And remember, when you are being tempted, do not say,
'God is tempting me.' God is never tempted to do wrong,
and he never tempts anyone else. Temptation comes
from our own desires, which entice us and drag us away.
These desires give birth to sinful actions. And when
sin is allowed to grow, it gives birth to death."
(James 1:13-15 NLT)

"What then? Shall we sin because we are not under law but under grace? Certainly not! Do you not know that to whom you present yourselves slaves to obey, you are that one's slaves whom you obey, whether of sin *leading* to death, or of obedience *leading* to righteousness? But God be thanked that you were slaves of sin, yet you obeyed from the heart that form of doctrine to which you were delivered. And having been set free from sin, you became slaves of righteousness."

(Romans 6:15-18)

Apostle Paul is sharing an inspired fundamental teaching: let our real estate be owned by God and not be of this world. If we allow the Holy Spirit to cleanse our minds, He brings forth rest for our troubled souls in the harshness of this world. We are to be immersed in the things of God. If we let Christ's mind be formed in us, we will know God's good and acceptable will. By allowing God to make us His holy possessions of righteousness, we let Christ rule in our hearts.

If you're new to understanding the Bible, you may be saying, "Why is Paul suggesting we are slaves? I don't want to be a slave. After all, didn't Jesus come to set me free?" Rightly so. The apostle Paul continues to say that he uses the term "slaves" to be able to relate to our carnal nature, to relate to how we can understand being bought with Christ's sacrifice.

Some people in those days were bought with a price if they had debt and could not pay it back. They could legally become a person's slave by law to pay off their debts for up to seven years. Slaves in those days were a little different than how we think of slavery today. It was more like a servant or as we understand butlers today. They helped around the house or yard or with one's business. They were a trustworthy employee who served the master of the house. In those days, people who were slaves were people who borrowed too much or stole goods and they could not pay it back, but after seven years were served, according to the law, they were legally set free regardless of if their debt was paid off or not.

But if the servant did not want to go because of the loyalty and care from the master, they could choose to serve the house of the master for life. They could choose to stay and be called a bondservant. Paul often starts his epistles calling himself "a bondservant of Christ," suggesting his debt was paid because of Jesus's blood, but now he has chosen to be a bondservant for good under the righteousness and love of Jesus. He wanted to be under the wings of Jesus and His protection, to be called a part of the kingdom of God. Paul was saying this in his humility and respect for God. Even though he was made a son of God, meaning heir, he was choosing to act in discipleship toward Christ and His will.

The carnal man cannot understand what is spiritual, but now we have a greater understanding of why one would want to be a "slave" of Christ. It is more an honour and privilege to be under one who is incorruptible, and it will result in security and protection.

If we are spiritual, then we can receive the things of God. Understanding this fundamental aspect will lead to fruit and discipleship. It reveals our hearts and minds. But if we bear bad fruit, we will be enslaved toward sin the master of this world, the devil. If we bear good fruit, we become loyal servants to thirst for righteousness (see Matthew 5:6). As bad fruit can bring forth issues in life that lead to turmoil, good fruit brings forth goodness, joy, and peace, just like the fruit of the spirit we covered before!

"But the natural man does not receive the things of the Spirit of God, for they are foolishness to him; nor can he know *them* because they are spiritually discerned."

(1 Corinthians 2:14)

Sharing the gospel can be a challenge sometimes. It's like as if you and the other person, are speaking two different languages! When people are in their carnal ways, they tend to think the message of the cross is foolish and meaningless, not discerning the spiritual application of the cross and the eternal salvation that comes with belief and repentance of sins.

As Christians, it's essential to understand that truth of patience. We were once dimmed to understanding the depth of the cross as well. But the message reached us. It can take time for unbelievers' minds to allow the Word of God in and their hearts to be filled with hope. Let the process of the Holy Spirit germinate. If we plant many seeds, it can take time for the seeds to grow and for the root systems to develop that can ultimately lead to labours of love. The message must be shared to enable people to have a chance to accept the truth.

The renewing of our mind is essential for our spiritual growth so we can share the gospel and have our roots grow deep and be confident in the truths we understand. If we receive the things of God, we can let our spirit man (the inner man of our soul) grow into the things of the Lord. We will soon cover how our souls are the temple of the Holy Spirit, which closely relates, but for now, I want you to understand that to become more spiritual is by the inner working of the Holy Spirit and His truths. To have the mind of Christ is a journey. Sometimes allowing Him in can be a struggle with our carnal nature as we covered how the flesh is at enmity with the Spirit. We need to let that old man die and let the new man live freely. The more we allow that to happen, the more we will have the inner thoughts of Christ. The old man's thoughts will become dimmed, and the lusts will soon fade away from desiring sin to desiring to love.

Sharing the gospel is like exercising our spirit man. Exercising and building muscles takes resistance; to be built in the spiritual world is to be trained in all different situations. The best way to penetrate the dimmed mind and fallen nature is to show grace and love exactly the way Jesus did for us. In fact, it is still through Jesus working and living inside of us on a daily basis that we receive His grace and grow.

To be more spiritual means to abide in Christ's love. In 1 Corinthians 13:2, the apostle Paul talks about how being more spiritual, at its very essence, is showing the love of God. He talks about how he can know all mysteries and knowledge, and he can have all faith to remove all issues in life, but he says that without love, he is like an annoying clanging cymbal. Biblical love is what germinates belief in Jesus in people's hearts. Sharing the good news of the gospel with love is the only way to reach people's dimmed minds and hardened hearts toward God. Then they will understand that love has made a way out from judgment of sin and wickedness. Let's explore the transforming power of love in-depth in the next chapter!

CHAPTER 8

The Power of Love with
The Temple of the Holy Spirit

"Now abide faith, hope, love, these three;
but the greatest of these *is* love."

(1 Corinthians 13:13)

I was preparing for a sermon one week, and I really wanted to illustrate the love of God and how powerful the gospel is. I remember thinking to myself, "What is the worst story I can find and show how Jesus turned it out for good?"

It was all about contrast to show God's saving power. How could I share a message to have a significant impact for my listeners? I found some documentaries about a cartel hitman who was called the "repo man."[6] [7] He was speaking about his past and how he did not care for his life, but he preferred to live for the gang called 18th Street in L.A. He killed many people and was notorious for his fearless approach. But the past caught up with this drug dealing

---

[6] "El Salvador's violent gang members are finding God in prison," YouTube video posted by The Economist, May 22, 2018, https://www.youtube.com/watch?v=7deancj6lzw.

[7] "Holy Murderers: El Salvador's Converted Criminals (Prison Documentary)," YouTube video posted by Real Stories, n.d., https://www.youtube.com/watch?v=_O6UeOT6mks

hitman, who got caught with many charges that caused him to be deported back to El Salvador, his birthplace.

When he arrived in his new El Salvador jail, he was angry, lost, and hurt. He had lost years of wealth relating to his illegal dealings. The affluent lifestyle he once lived became a cell block that he shared with over one hundred other inmates hanging in hammocks above one another, all the way to the high ceiling. When he first arrived at that jail, he shares that there had recently been a massacre of gang members by other inmates. It had caused large riots, and guards had to stop everyone from killing one another with force. He shared that he could still smell all the blood that had recently been cleaned.

He contracted an infection that was common in low-standard living conditions. In first-world countries, it can be treated, but at this prison, gang members ran the jail inside, and there were just the guards on watchtowers with automatic rifles to kill anyone trying to escape. Let's say the medical treatment was hard to come by.

He accepted that he had maybe about three years to live with tuberculosis. Jesus was planting a few small seeds of love in a group of Christians in this jail. The small group of believers developed over time, and this number increased as the seeds of the gospel were shared. When a Christian man saw this man in need, he went up to this hardened hitman to pray for his tuberculosis to be healed. The "repo man" accepted the prayer. The next day, he was healed. He could now breathe without hearing the blood in his chest fill up at night. Jesus showed mercy and grace to this murderer. The Christian asked if he would accept Jesus as his saviour, and the repo man accepted Jesus right then as his saviour. He now believed, and the grace of God was just about to unfold in that prison.

The Christian group began to grow in great numbers. The more hardened criminals poured through the prison gates with the usual high turnover rate from all different gangs in South America, the more the love of Christ was poured out into the inmates' hearts.

It got to a stage where this jail of a few multiplied to fifty then one hundred and then three hundred. After not too long, the prison was majority Christian with more than one thousand believers! Many new arrivals saw the paradigm change. Many were young, hurting men who were lost in a war driven by excess drugs, greed, and gang pride. The repo man understood these young men were the same as him; under the death-provoked tattoos and bloodlust was a young boy who was hurt and discouraged. The gospel turned these hardened hearts into flesh; they were changed and welcomed by the love and acceptance of Jesus Christ. Redemption gave them a second chance, and hope was given to these men through Jesus's sacrifice on cross. Although many gang members still had years to serve for the crimes they had committed, to God they were cleansed, free and holy in God's eyes, redeemed by Christ. The paradigm of the prison changed, and the guards were no longer required to use the brutal force they were once accustomed to.

Jesus turned that jail from having seeds of hate germinating into the bad fruits of death to having seeds of love scattered and sown. It revealed a swift change to spiritual blessing and love songs unto Jesus all day. There were Bible studies around the clock. The ex-hitman is now the head pastor at that church in prison, and he now preaches repentance of sin by the blood of Jesus. He believes Jesus will turn around the gang crimes and use some of the most hardened criminals as revivalists to the nations. Jesus and the seeds of love from the gospel can turn the hardest people into the kindest people full of love by the renewing power of the mind of Christ and the acceptance of the cross to all people—all.

> "'I have not come to call *the* righteous,
> but sinners, to repentance.'"
>
> (Luke 5:32)

We are the temple

> "Do you not know that your body is the temple of the Holy Spirit *who is* in you, whom you have from God?"
>
> (1 Corinthians 6:19)

Do you know that we are the temple of the living God? Jesus indwells us with His Holy Spirit. The gang members we covered are born again, and their sins are now forgiven, yet they still have gang-related tattoos all over their bodies. In this life, we all have reminders of our past. It is so important to gain knowledge from the Word of God and to live by faith. We need to trust Jesus that we are new creations ... born again, revived, cleansed because of His love toward us.

God shares in His Word about how He has made all things new and old things have passed away (see 2 Corinthians 5:17). The convicted criminals have the past constantly reminding them of who they once were each time they look at their death tattoos in the mirror or wake up in their jail cell. But it's not how Christ sees them now. He sees them as His new creation, and since He sees them that way, it's essential to understand that they have a renewed mind and heart. God has declared them holy and ready to be His temple of His Holy Spirit.

They are born again; they are the temple of the living God now! Jesus reveals His immense love through His sacrifice that cleansed them. Their outward appearance had symbolic tattoos of death and stories of murder in their ink. Yet they are white as snow because Jesus is alive! We were once marked like these criminals, but in our minds, and our souls were marked as sinners towards God (see Colossians 1:21). We were all sinners to God and had fallen short of His holiness (see Romans 3:23).

If we have broken one commandment, we have broken them all (see James 2:10). It's like if we are hanging over the edge of a cliff gripping onto a chain, but then the top link in the chain starts to bend and break. Can the other unbroken links save us? No. It only requires one link in the chain to break for us to fall. That's how God sees His law; if we break one, we are considered transgressors of all.

"For whoever shall keep the whole law, and yet stumble in one *point*, he is guilty of all. For He who said, 'Do not commit adultery,' also said, 'Do not murder.' Now if you do not commit adultery, but you do murder, you have become a transgressor of the law."

(James 2:10-11)

The resurrection power of the blood of Jesus makes us able to house the gift of the Holy Spirit and to be called the temple of the living God. Our sins were many, but we have been made white as snow!

"'Come now, and let us reason together,'
Says the LORD,
'Though your sins are like scarlet,
They shall be as white as snow;
Though they are red like crimson,
They shall be as wool.'"

(Isaiah 1:18)

In the Old Testament temple, there were cleansing ceremonies required in order to enter into the holy of holies. That was the inner part of the temple where the ark of the covenant and mercy seat of God were.

The high priest was only allowed to enter the most holy place one time a year, on Yom Kippur, which means "day of atonement," for remission of sins for the people. The high priest was to offer a sacrifice of a bullock and to release a goat also known as the "scapegoat." The high priest was in new fine plain linen and was required to bathe and be clean before entering and to be humble before God. There had to be sweet incense burning in the room so the smoke would fill the space so the sinful eyes of the high priest were hidden from God and His holiness as God cannot look upon sin (see Habakkuk 1:13).

The holy of holies was separated from the rest of the temple by the veil, a massive drape made of fine linen and purple, blue, and scarlet yarn and embroidered with gold cherubim. To enter behind the veil into the holy of holies was a significant yet fearful event held to cover the sins of the Israelites each year.

Often the high priest had bells on his robe and a small rope attached to his ankle so another priest could hear the high priest walking in the inner holy sanctuary. The rope was there to pull his body out if he had sinned or did something wrong in the holy of holies. The righteousness of God could not allow His temple to be defiled, and if the priest had failed to be cleansed or did something wrong in God's eyes, he would be struck dead by God's holy presence. [8] It's awesome to see the contrast of God's Love that was given to us, now we are the temple of the Holy Spirit. To see the power of Jesus working in that prison, goes to show the extent of the power of Jesus' blood that now makes us holy through faith. It's good to see God's perspective of His Holiness and the extreme measures that were required in the Old Covenant, but now to see the New and Better Convent, and it's supreme blessing of Holiness being outworked in people's lives.

To have a holy fear and awe of God is healthy. Wisdom starts when we have a fear of God as we will cover near the end of the book (see Proverbs 9:10). After all, He is the creator of the universe and has all power in His hands to execute what He wills. When Jesus went to the cross, He separated that veil that was between us. He removed the sin

---

[8] Robert Jamieson, "How the high priest must enter into the holy place," https://biblehub.com/library/jamieson/commentary_ critical_and_explanatory_on_the_whole_bible/le_16_1- 34_how_the_high.htm, Aug. 4, 2022.

that was stopping the love of God from being poured into our hearts.

"The love of God has been poured out in our hearts by the Holy Spirit who was given to us."

(Romans 5:5)

The veil has been ripped down the middle (see Matthew 27:51). When Jesus was on the cross, He fulfilled all the types and shadows that the prophets had displayed from the Holy Spirit. The Holy Spirit sent His prophets in times past to show the acts of love that He would display to His people as a sign of the Messiah.

The suffering Messiah was revealed throughout the Bible for thousands of years and forty different authors. The Bible always had a central message, and that is Jesus Christ.

The veil had not been lifted until Christ fulfilled the law of God and the mystery was revealed. Sin was dealt with, and when one believes in Christ, the veil from the Old Testament text is removed so we can see with understanding to repent and believe in Jesus Christ as the Messiah (see 2 Corinthians 3:14).

The holy tabernacle on earth was a type and shadow of things to come. A type or shadow means a display of a figure, or event, that has yet to be fulfilled to show the fingerprint of God and how He shapes the future and can see future events before they happen. These are used to reveal His plans to the prophets and for the people to see God's hand working to know it is Him.

Revelation 21:22 talks about there being no holy temple in New Jerusalem because God Himself is the holy temple. The Bible talks about how we are to abide in Christ and live in Him. The terminology of the Bible shares that we are built as blocks of stones of the holy temple, and Christ is the cornerstone. The church is built on His foundation for an eternal dwelling place of worship and love.

When we can see the love that He has given us and the holiness of God, we can see the true gift of eternal salvation and the right we have to be filled with His Holy Spirit, which once hovered abundantly within the holy of holies. We can experience the power of the blood of Jesus through His sanctifying power, as we will cover in the next few chapters!

CHAPTER 9

Be Set Apart

As we are temples of God and the Holy Spirit abides within us, Paul talks about how God wants His people to live in this temporary world, let idols be far from us, and live holy lifestyles unto the Lord.

"What agreement has the temple of God with idols? For you are the temple of the living God. As God has said:

"'I will dwell in them
And walk among *them*.
I will be their God,
And they shall be My people.'

"Therefore

"'Come out from among them
And be separate, says the Lord.
Do not touch what is unclean,
And I will receive you.'
'I will be a Father to you,
And you shall be My sons and daughters,
Says the LORD Almighty.'"

(2 Corinthians 6:16-18)

Being separate from the world can have its challenges. Still, the apostle Paul is not saying not to associate with people around you or to be isolated. Instead, what he is saying is to let the lust of the flesh be gone and do not consent with the world. For example, many movies are indulgent of the flesh and darkened content from blinded minds can be projected on our TVs that can feed our minds and can try to draw us away from the holiness of God through us drifting back into darkness.

Now I'm not saying don't watch TV or movies; this is just an example of the massive exposure sin has to the world in this current generation. So we must take guard on what we allow to enter our minds. For example, we wouldn't grieve the Holy Spirit by going to a strip club or watching violent fighting in different corners of the world, would we? So why subject our minds to ungodly behaviour just because it's displayed on screens through actors' lives?

The human mind can easily be conditioned. We have never had the reality that TV offers now in all of our human existence. The snares of conditioning lead to sin, and the doors once hidden behind bouncers and dark places in the middle of the night are now one click away from our unmonitored living rooms and being constantly flashed before our faces. It's so easy to be conditioned by constant bombardment of these so-called realities that can shape and form our mindsets.

We are now made holy as decreed by God. Jesus wants us to be set apart with Him in integrity, in mind and spirit; to stand up for what is right; to be walking in His truths; and to be the light and salt of the world and share His ways with love. He wants us to live for God and to be a living holy temple, to have modesty and patience, and be clothed with peace. He wants our bodies to be homes for the Holy Spirit, so He can lead and direct our lives for His purposes, to edify and lift one another up, to be a sweet-smelling aroma of the knowledge of Christ to others, to live unto God, to walk blameless before Him in love, and to be amenable.

Since the world has been corrupted, God wants to protect what is His and be separated from the fallen ideology of life. We have an inheritance from the King of Kings to be set apart. It is a blessing to have His Holy Spirit living within us. We see in the Scriptures in the Old Testament that wherever the ark of the covenant was, God's favour and blessings followed (see 2 Samuel 6:11-15). We have royalty living within us to help enrich our lives through spiritual grace. The holy tabernacle/temple was made with the finest materials for God to dwell within—for our sakes, to have Him near us. We now can have a close and intimate relationship with the Father because of His Son, Jesus. It's good to see the Old Testament temple in Scripture and to appreciate the holiness that we now have for the Holy Spirit to able to live within us. As was covered before briefly about the fear of God, sometimes we can underestimate the holiness of God and our old human state of rebellion can easily blind us. For the Holy Spirit to live in us reveals the power of Christ's blood.

Jesus wants us to be perfecting holiness with the fear of God and to let our minds agree with what is acceptable and holy as we are housing the Holy Spirit. It's no small thing for such a gift to be given, and as we grow in grace with Jesus, we can learn of His riches toward us. Christ reveals His care for us in building an intimate relationship by His

Holy Spirit. We can treasure Him by seeking after His will and allowing His Holy Spirit to show His sanctifying power within our lives. When we grow with Jesus, we can yearn for His ways that open reality for the greater eternal home. Being set apart can have its challenges, but once we have tasted that the Lord is good, we will be thirsty for His kingdom and the fruits of peace that follow.

Many people in the Bible we have read about have been sojourners simply passing through to a better world and to receive far greater eternal rewards. They lost much here and were persecuted, but they had joy and a prospect of Christ's love to empower them into seeking God's kingdom over this world's fading pleasures.

Being set apart can be applied in this manner; we can know that this life is not the be-all and end-all. Although it is best to make the most of this world, we cannot take anything out of it—well, besides the rewards of serving Jesus! So, it makes sense that God wants us to be set apart and do good with what we have and share the good news. Christ can be our treasure. It's great to be able to share that with others and let the family of Jesus grow into maturity and to have all things in common with each other. The Holy Spirit is the bond of peace within us, and a self-reflecting Christian should allow those attributes to flow freely for unity with brothers and sisters in the Lord.

There's nothing better than having brothers and sisters who dwell in harmony. That is precisely what God wants. The Bible is clear that where there is unity, God commands the blessings (see Psalm 133). His church is to be holy, set apart, and have all things in common.

"Now the multitude of those who believed were of
one heart and one soul; neither did anyone say that
any of the things he possessed was his own, but they
had all things in common."

(Acts 4:32)

Being a Christian can be a lonely walk. Not all allow the
Holy Spirit to flow as He should, and having division within
the church can be heartbreaking and discouraging. It's
common for people who do not believe to misunderstand
and mistreat Christians because many are blinded by the
ruler of this world, Satan (see 2 Corinthians 4:4). He can use
that to persecute the church.

But as Christians, it's so important that we can get
together and have fellowship with one another in the bond
of Christ. We can feel a part of His family, which has all
things in common. Christ is the foundation of that. Living in
the world and enjoying the world can be challenging, so we
need one another to help build our faith and to encourage
each other as a community. The hardness of the world can
often grieve the Holy Spirit, but to be set apart is a process
that the Holy Spirit can use to build us up and help us
become fruit bearers for Christ's name. Let's go to the story
of Lot and how he was a believer yet refused to be set apart
and was daily grieved by the wickedness of Sodom.

"Righteous Lot … *was* oppressed by the filthy conduct
of the wicked (for that righteous man, dwelling among
them, tormented *his* righteous soul from day to day by
seeing and hearing *their* lawless deeds)."

(2 Peter 2:6-8)

God turned the cities of Sodom and Gomorrah into ashes, condemned them to destruction, making them an example to those who afterward would live ungodly; and delivered righteous Lot, who was oppressed by the filthy conduct of the wicked. Sodom and Gomorrah are a representation of the kingdom of darkness. Lawlessness and hate toward God can cause an indulgence of idolised fallen passions that lead to wickedness and sin.

Lot wanted to live in Sodom. He wanted to have the security of the city and walls, the ease of community living and busy marketplaces full of fresh produce. He resisted the idea of leaving the city when he heard God would destroy it.

Ultimately, he did leave, but that meant he had to give away his lifestyle. Even though he was righteous before God and the acts of the wicked city grieved his soul daily, he still chose to tolerate the wicked acts. He did not want to be set apart but chose the things of this world and the pleasures that can come along with it. It's a story God has taught His people. Although Lot lived in an ungodly society, it did not make him unrighteous, but it was a struggle for him to have anything in common with people who were darkened because of sin. Dark and light cannot meet. There will always be conflicting issues like magnet forces trying to push away from each other. Abraham, Lot's uncle, influenced Lot and his love for the true and living God.

Abraham spoke to the Lord after He announced that He would destroy Sodom and Gomorrah because of the cries the Lord heard from people who were affected by the wicked cities. Abraham asked the Lord to not destroy the cities if just ten righteous people were living within the walls (out of hundreds of thousands of people). The Lord agreed to the request (see Genesis 18:32), but the Lord did not find ten righteous, but only around three to four who were of Lot's household.

It reveals the worth that God has on those who seek His uprightness. The Lord would spare judgment on half a million wicked people who were murderers and idolators for ten who were upright. The value the Lord places on His people is truly amazing. Unfortunately, Lot chose to be unequally yoked with unbelievers, and his family were not fully blessed. The Lord sent angels to lead Lot out. His family were commanded not to look back at the fire coming from the heavens to declare God's anger with the wicked city. Unfortunately, Lot's wife looked back and was turned to salt (see Genesis 19).

Abraham and Lot had much land and livestock. They were both very wealthy from the Lord. The parallel here is when Abraham told Lot to choose what side of land he wanted because they were too abundant to live next to each other with their herds. Lot decided to go separate ways from his uncle, and the fellowship they shared was a great loss for both.

Lot admired and looked up to Abraham. Lot chose to live with ungodly people, yet he did not fall away from God. It was an example showing the parallelism of one who chooses to be a sojourner and to seek the higher things of God or the torment of this short life with having a part with unbelievers and the actions that grieved the soul of Lot and the Holy Spirit daily. Lot was unequally yoked with unbelievers, and it had its benefits for some things, but spiritually and morally, it was very hard for him.

"Do not be unequally yoked together with unbelievers. For what fellowship has righteousness with lawlessness? And what communion has light with darkness? And what accord has Christ with Belial? Or what part has a believer with an unbeliever? And what agreement has the temple of God with idols?"

(2 Corinthians 6:14-16)

On the flipside, Abraham was a sojourner on this land living in a foreign land, residing in tents and being led by the Spirit of God. Abraham was looking for the reward of the eternal foundations made by God. He was looking to the better promises. Abraham was an example of a believer who shared his God and lived and obeyed the Lord—not that Lot was disobedient, but Lot was possibly unequally yoked and lost all that he had invested in Sodom. Abraham had an abundance of favour with God. Abraham's heart was for heaven and not for earth. He was not unequally yoked with unbelievers, although he had his trials and tribulations and his faith was tested. But once his faith was tested, he was a vessel of gold worthy for God's house.

"But in a great house there are not only vessels of gold and silver, but also of wood and clay, some for honor and some for dishonor. Therefore if anyone cleanses himself from the latter, he will be a vessel for honor, sanctified and useful for the Master, prepared for every good work. Flee also youthful lusts; but pursue righteousness, faith, love, peace with those who call on the Lord out of a pure heart."

(2 Timothy 2:20-22)

To be set apart means to be holy and having put away the things of the old man, to be made a special instrument of righteousness for the Lord. As the apostle is teaching young Timothy, a great house has many different types of housewares, and each set has a unique and different function for honour or dishonour.

God wants believers to leave behind the world's ways and to be set apart for His use in this world to reveal the character of Jesus in us as His fingerprint of love. God is showing us as believers there are eternal rewards of honour for those who seek God's righteousness and put Him first in what they do. We are to cleanse ourselves from the latter ways of life by the empowerment of the Holy Spirit working in our lives for good to train and to equip us for His ministry of love.

CHAPTER 10

The Power of the Blood

The transformation power of the blood of Jesus is so evident spiritually. What was defiled and sinful then becomes white as snow, as we covered with the gang members. That's what Jesus does! If there is hope for them, there is hope for anyone! All of our sins are forgiven and forgotten. Just like how the Lord would spare millions of sinners for ten righteous, for Christ who is perfect and blameless, it was the Father's will who declare us innocent before Him because of the blood of Jesus and how He paid our debt.

Let's look at the court system briefly: a judge can dismiss a fine if we have someone else pay for us if it's a mutual agreement between the person paying and the person who has the debt. The judge does not care if that arrangement is done or not, as long as the fine is paid. Likewise, Jesus has paid our debts through His blood on the cross. If we accept the gift from Jesus in a mutual understanding with thanks, we can trust He is faithful and will pay what was needed. It is lawful for God to allow that to happen for our sins because of a legal technicality that first allowed sin into the world, as we will cover below!

Adam was the first man, and Jesus is the second Adam, and since one man's sin allowed sin into the world, it is just and right for one man's righteousness to take the sins of the world away (see 1 Corinthians 15:45–49 and Romans 5:12-19).

> "There is a natural body, and there is a spiritual body.
> And so it is written, "The first man Adam became a living
> being." The last Adam *became* a life-giving spirit."
>
> (1 Corinthians 15:44-45)

> "He Himself is the propitiation for our sins, and
> not for ours only but also for the whole world."
>
> (1 John 2:2)

God's ways are manifold, and a way that seemed impossible was made possible only by the Father accepting Christ as the atonement (Yom Kippur) to remove sin from all people of the faith. It is just that if one man can allow sin into this world, then one man can give eternal life in the world by His perfect life offered freely for us. The mutual agreement is between us and Jesus to accept the gift that He eagerly wants us to accept. His blood covers our debts, and now we have Jesus as our high priest who entered the spiritual temple to take away the sins of the people who turn to Him. He has offered Himself at the end of the ages to be a final payment for all who believe.

The Father accepted Jesus's legal payment of sin through one man, Jesus. The Bible shares those sins' wages are death, but the gift of God is eternal life because of our Passover Christ!

"For when you were slaves of sin, you were free in regard to righteousness. What fruit did you have then in the things of which you are now ashamed? For the end of those things *is* death. But now having been set free from sin, and having become slaves of God, you have your fruit to holiness, and the end, everlasting life. For the wages of sin *is* death, but the gift of God *is* eternal life in Christ Jesus our Lord."

(Romans 6:20-23)

When we are made perfect by the blood of Jesus, our debts are paid, but you may be asking why did Jesus have to die and why was His blood so important? What's the significance of the blood of Jesus or blood in general? The Bible talks about life in the blood.

""For the life of the flesh *is* in the blood, and I have given it to you upon the altar to make atonement for your souls; for it *is* the blood *that* makes atonement for the soul."""

(Leviticus 17:11)

The Bible talks about how bull and goat sacrifices were enough to cover people's sins, but animals' blood never removed sin. It could cover sins, but not remove sins.

That is the power of Jesus. His sacrifice was there to remove sins for an eternal purpose. As God gave Adam a covering in the garden of Eden after he sinned, it was a covering of his nakedness and sin. Well, Jesus Christ is the removal of all impurities by His holy and pure sacrifice. Jesus fulfilled all the Old Testament commandments, the old covenant promises that God gave, so a New Testament could come into place.

105

Instead of the law that brought death from our sin, Jesus brought a law of love and liberty. Since Christ fulfilled the Father's laws perfectly, it ushered in a New Testament promise of peace and grace for His people and all who will be willing to accept His gift of mercy for the remission of sins.

"For where there *is* a testament, there must also of necessity be the death of the testator. For a testament *is* in force after men are dead, since it has no power at all while the testator lives. Therefore not even the first *covenant* was dedicated without blood. For when Moses had spoken every precept to all the people according to the law, he took the blood of calves and goats, with water, scarlet wool, and hyssop, and sprinkled both the book itself and all the people, saying, 'This *is* the blood of the covenant which God has commanded you.' Then likewise he sprinkled with blood both the tabernacle and all the vessels of the ministry. And according to the law almost all things are purified with blood, and without shedding of blood there is no remission."

(Hebrews 9:16-22)

Interesting stuff: Jesus is the new testator!! That's why He needed to die. He is our new high priest who has been rewarded in the holy of holies to sit on the mercy seat at the right hand of the Father (Yahweh). That's excellent news, as the Bible talks about how we have a high priest who can sympathise with us, who also lived in a fallen world, and He understands what we go through, but now we have access to Him from His sacrifice, which tore down the veil for us so we can now be in fellowship with the Father though our high priest, Christ!

"Therefore, brethren, having boldness to enter the Holiest by the blood of Jesus, by a new and living way which He consecrated for us, through the veil, that is, His flesh, and *having* a High Priest over the house of God, let us draw near with a true heart in full assurance of faith, having our hearts sprinkled from an evil conscience and our bodies washed with pure water. Let us hold fast the confession of *our* hope without wavering, for He who promised *is* faithful."

(Hebrews 10:19-23)

That is the power of the blood of Jesus. It is access to the holiest place, and we are made pure and holy before God so the Holy Spirit can intercede on our behalf.

At the start of this book, I said that love is on every page of the Bible. With understanding, growth, and maturity, it truly is. We can form a fellowship with the Holy Spirit. The intimacy of His love and the cultivation by the Holy Spirit cleanses our hearts toward God by faith in the blood of Jesus. The more we understand, the more we can see the true selfless love God has given to His people over thousands of years. It is in our best interest to search for treasures of knowledge and to be led by His Spirit to allow the benefits of having the veil removed so that we can see God's personality of love through the divine actions He has done and the prophecies that have been fulfilled.

It's my main objective to help to explain to give more context and hopefully allow better understanding that can help nurture your spiritual growth. I will cover a short commentary on Isaiah 53 below, but first let's read the prophet's inspired words and how the Holy Spirit develops His Word to allow us to understand his message. There is no substitute for time in the Bible and the power of the Holy Spirit that can guide our paths. Let the Word of God open your hearts in greater depth. Many Christians do not read their Bibles as often as they should. In many ways, it can be overlooked, and with this fast-paced life and with great speakers, at times we feel we don't need to, but the Word of God is manifold, and revelations can come the more we seek His knowledge. Doing so results in spiritual fertiliser for growth to our inner man.

Each time I look in the Bible, Jesus shows me more revelation of His love and acts that He planned through His mercy and grace. Here's the Word of God to see God's heart of love for us as He was beaten, mocked, and sacrificed by His own will for our benefit. His blood has brought healing in our mortal bodies; His blood has brought us peace by His chastisement and purchased many souls to be able to enter the kingdom of God.

Isaiah 53

"Who has believed our report?
And to whom has the arm of the LORD been revealed?
For He shall grow up before Him as a tender plant,
And as a root out of dry ground.
He has no form or comeliness;
And when we see Him,
There is no beauty that we should desire Him.
He is despised and rejected by men,

A Man of sorrows and acquainted with grief.
And we hid, as it were, *our* faces from Him;
He was despised, and we did not esteem Him.

"Surely He has borne our griefs
And carried our sorrows;
Yet we esteemed Him stricken,
Smitten by God, and afflicted.
But He *was* wounded for our transgressions,
He was bruised for our iniquities;
The chastisement for our peace *was* upon Him,
And by His stripes we are healed.
All we like sheep have gone astray;
We have turned, every one, to his own way;
And the LORD has laid on Him the iniquity of us all.

"He was oppressed and He was afflicted,
Yet He opened not His mouth;
He was led as a lamb to the slaughter,
And as a sheep before its shearers is silent,
So He opened not His mouth.
He was taken from prison and from judgment,
And who will declare His generation?
For He was cut off from the land of the living;
For the transgressions of My people He was stricken.
And they made His grave with the wicked—
But with the rich at His death,
Because He had done no violence,
Nor *was any* deceit in His mouth.

"Yet it pleased the LORD to bruise Him;
He has put *Him* to grief.
When You make His soul an offering for sin,
He shall see *His* seed, He shall prolong *His* days,
And the pleasure of the LORD shall prosper in His hand.
He shall see the labor of His soul, *and* be satisfied.
By His knowledge My righteous Servant shall justify many,
For He shall bear their iniquities.
Therefore I will divide Him a portion with the great,
And He shall divide the spoil with the strong,
Because He poured out His soul unto death,
And He was numbered with the transgressors,
And He bore the sin of many,
And made intercession for the transgressors."

In Isaiah, the prophet was prophetically speaking about who will believe in the mercy that Jesus has given to us from the cross and resurrection power. The Bible talks about few who find the narrow path that leads to the kingdom of heaven through belief and repentance, but wide is the gate that leads to destruction (see Matthew 7:13-14).

Many people are in unbelief towards a simple, yet powerful act of love that Jesus has achieved. Belief is important with God. He will not give His salvation to those who do not believe. Not believing in what God has said or done is an act of calling God a liar or saying He is not true. It reveals an unrepentant heart and a love for sin over God and a self-righteous attitude that we don't need Him.

We have evidence of Him everywhere, with the creation of the world as we covered before. Jesus can judge us off that knowledge and the moral law within our minds, yet so many people resist the good report. Jesus told a parable about a rich man who lived a wealthy lifestyle who had no time for the things of God but indulged in unrighteous living and mistreated people. Jesus depicts that this man was in hell, and he was begging Abraham for just a simple drop of water. Abraham was in the depths of the earth as well, but in the righteous resting place on the other side of the gulf that no one could pass (see Luke 16:19-31).

The righteous had to be placed there because the animal sacrifice had not purified their souls to be with God in His holy place. Before Jesus was crucified, they believed in the Lord by faith. He had not been fully revealed until the gospel had taken place. Jesus had to die and rise again for all the souls who were on the good side of Sheol so they could be released into the kingdom of heaven with God. First came the natural, then the supernatural. As He said on the cross, it is finished. The Bible talks about how the tabernacle was a type and shadow of the actual temple in heaven where Jesus is high priest. His blood was sprinkled on the mercy seat for the redemptions of our sins and to be made in right standing with God.

In the parable of the man asking for a drop of water, the man then asks Abraham to send one back from the dead to share with his household about the realities of hell. Abraham said they have Moses and the prophets, but no one believes their report. If no one will believe their word, neither will they believe if one comes back from the dead to testify. We see the parallelism everywhere over the Bible and the general unbelief of people—even if one is raised from death (Christ), still people refuse to repent and believe.

God gives many chances to all, but if they do not believe, how can God sway them to repent? He gave so much evidence for His resurrection if we search for it. The facts are mind-blowing. Check out Lee Strobel's *The Case for Christ* book. He covers that in great detail.

Jesus's blood will not remove people's sins who are in hell because they rejected the report while on earth. As we are all eternal, after we die, we have to go somewhere. God has no choice for sinners to go to hell in judgment. Hell was never made for humans, rather only Satan and his demons (see Matthew 25:41), but if a man agrees to sin and agrees with Satan's will of rebellion, humans also will be put in the lake of fire.

Jesus left nothing undone for us. He has shown His love for mankind since the start. Yet He is holy and righteous, and He has also dealt with us in times just like a father chastens his children, but as the Bible said, He prefers mercy over judgment (see James 2:13). So, Jesus preferred mercy for us, that He would be the debt payer, so He would become as sin for us and His blood would be the atonement. What more could we ask for than that God would demonstrate this love? He laid down His life for us so we can receive a wonderful gift of salvation with power from His blood to make us valued and beloved heirs of Christ.

Isaiah offers a great depth of insight into the details of the cross and His love and the power of belief. Jesus was led to the slaughter for mankind, and He was humble enough not to turn His face nor open his mouth, but He endured the punishment and wrath of God for the propitiation of our sins!

"Who *is* a God like You,
Pardoning iniquity
And passing over the transgression of the remnant of His heritage?

"He does not retain His anger forever,
Because He delights *in* mercy.
He will again have compassion on us,
And will subdue our iniquities.

"You will cast all our sins
Into the depths of the sea."

(Micah 7:18-19)

The Bible never advocated human sacrifices. It was always animals for the sacrifice as a type for Jesus to be the perfect sinless lamb, to take away the world's reproaches through faith and belief in Him. As humans, we can think about human sacrifices, and it seems so wrong and not loving if we were to do that to one of our own for any reason. The Bible has been clear that it was essential for our sins to be removed entirely and forgotten. It was not of our will, rather the Father's gift to mankind. In the next chapter, let's explore the greatest love story ever recorded, and the patience, forgiveness, and outstretched arm the Lord has for His bride-to-be.

CHAPTER 11

A Love Story That Entails a Bride and a Groom

Suppose there is the most incredible love story in history. The Bible certainly reveals it in God's faithfulness to His betrothed love. The Bible shares with us God's relationship with humans over thousands of years: a love conceived before time began; a love story of hurt, human betrayal, longsuffering, godly loyalty, victory, and honour; a foundation of forgiveness, a foundation of truth and peace, and an authentic happily ever after.

This is what is revealed in the Bible over thousands of years. There is a bride who has been madly in love with her Creator, with a bond stronger than any human emotion can reveal, but as time ticks on, past events and generations slowly become replaced by the new. Past family trees can remember no further than their grandparents' faithful memories of His heroic saving right hand. Over and over again, the Saviour reveals His love, mercy, and grace to thousands of new generations to share His betrothed love with His people, but sometimes, they lose their way and can become reclusive toward the groom's precious love and become stagnant as human loyalty fades like a flower in the hot dry summer sun. Rebellion attacks their camps at these times to cause abominations and for God to reveal judgment for their own good so they can be placed back on the path of life.

God never stops revealing His love through His wondrous saving right hand that ignites the flame for the next generation to be witnesses. This tells a story of longsuffering, patience, and the human fallen condition that has been made right by redemption through the blood of Jesus for His beloved bride-to-be.

God has revealed Himself to His beloved over thousands of years through the prophets, who are ambassadors to declare His ministry of judgment or love. God reveals His heart to the prophets so they can deliver different tasks and instructions to let His people know the plans He has for them. It's a way that God communicates to His people.

When God's people are going astray, He raises a prophet or prophets to warn, to rebuke, and to give options before there is judgment. One of the events I want to illustrate is the prophet Hosea and the typology of Jesus. It is covered all over the Bible, but let's focus in on Hosea after a quick rundown of some history of Israel to help understand the judgment in the book of Hosea.

Israel had been in abundance after the reigns of King David and King Solomon. There had never been such a time of peace in the last 250 years of their history. They had blessing and abundance from the likes of King David, who was fierce and full of integrity. He led Israel to victory. He was a type of Christ who was to come. But often, as time goes by in this mortal life, leadership changes, and things of the past do not stay the same.

Israel had benefited from the fruitful kingdom God gave King David, but Solomon strayed in his later years, following after foreign gods. God began to take the kingdom away after Solomon had died. Still, God remained faithful to one tribe for the sake of King David's loyalty. Now back to the book of Hosea.

Hosea's name translates to the name Joshua, and in modern times, the name also closely relates with Jesus over a few different languages. Hosea, Joshua, Jesus: all these names interrelate meanings of the saviour, salvation, and God who saves. [9]

After the prosperity in the land, God brought a stern judgment on His people after leaving the Lord for abundance. They forgot the Lord and chose to follow the idols they had made.

They became harlots, or for a modern term prostitutes, and strayed from God. This book of Hosea is fundamentally based on the sins of Israel and their unfaithfulness toward the Lord. The people of God had left their first love and run after other gods that they had created to serve their desires of sin.

"'The more they increased,
The more they sinned against Me;
I will change their glory into shame.
They eat up the sin of My people;
They set their heart on their iniquity.'"

(Hosea 4:7-8)

---

9 "Hebrew Word of the Day," Jerusalem Prayer Team,
https://hebrew.jerusalemprayerteam.org/yeshua-jesus-joshua-hosea/,
Aug. 4, 2022.

They had become murderers, thieves, and liars, committing sexual sins and worshipping false gods made by man. They had become dull of the ways of God and chose to rebel. God illustrates to Hosea to be a type of Christ. He was to essentially live with the actions that Israel had been doing toward God. We will look at the Scripture below that gave his instructions:

"When the LORD began to speak by Hosea,
the LORD said to Hosea:
'Go, take yourself a wife of harlotry
And children of harlotry,
For the land has committed great harlotry
By *departing* from the LORD.'"

(Hosea 1:2)

God wanted Hosea to take a prostitute as a wife. In our modern times, doing that would create a challenging circumstance to live with and to accept. On a fundamental level of privacy and trust, it would be emotional with ups and downs that came with the stigma of marrying a prostitute and her promiscuous ways (see Hosea 1:2, Hosea 3:1).

In Hosea's time, that decision would have been unthinkable in society. A prophet with a prostitute would have been habitually mocked by the public, religious leaders and the priests of God. Yet God was making a stern point that the religious leaders and priests were also in the same sins and traps as the nation of Israel. God wanted Hosea to take a prostitute as a wife and to be a public spectacle to His people as they were being like a harlot toward God.

"'And it shall be: like people, like priest.
So I will punish them for their ways,
And reward them for their deeds.
For they shall eat, but not have enough;
They shall commit harlotry, but not increase;
Because they have ceased obeying the LORD.'"

(Hosea 4:9-10)

It had come to a point when God thought it best to bring judgment on His people, who He had chosen for Himself; even the holy priests were to be judged. It shows us the decay and how disobedient Israel had become with the lavish lifestyles and riches they had. They thought God approved of their lifestyles of sin because of their abundance. But it was to become judgment, and God revealed their actions as their story was acted out before them with Hosea and his wife.

Although the judgment was imminent toward the people of Israel, and especially toward the northern tribes who fell away from God, we see in the Scriptures that God is longsuffering and faithful to Israel. Even though He had proclaimed judgment and that He would curse them for their disobedience, He still had mercy on them to give a glimmer of hope.

"'Therefore, behold, I will allure her,
Will bring her into the wilderness,
And speak comfort to her.'"

(Hosea 2:14)

The Lord, in His judgment, had said that He would bring Israel to himself and comfort her. He would give judgement that He had proclaimed to the north of Israel, but in the south, He said He would continue His covenant with Judah for the line of king David's sake.

"'I will betroth you to Me forever;
Yes, I will betroth you to Me
In righteousness and justice,
In lovingkindness and mercy;
I will betroth you to Me in faithfulness,
And you shall know the LORD.'"

(Hosea 2:19-20)

As His people were like harlots, Hosea married a prostitute. Hosea's wife was continually unfaithful to him. God told Hosea to remain faithful, to give her gifts, and to show her love. This is what God was doing with the people of the tribe Judah. His love, longsuffering, and patience toward her was steadfast, and he committed to working out issues.

"Come, and let us return to the LORD;
For He has torn, but He will heal us;
He has stricken, but He will bind us up.
After two days He will revive us;
On the third day He will raise us up,
That we may live in His sight."

(Hosea 6:1-2)

Jesus was raised on the third day to make alive and revive the people from the sins of Israel, not only the sins of Israel but the entire world who would believe in the good report because of the rejection of Israel. It meant riches for the gentiles (see Romans 11:12).

"'Then I will sow her for Myself in the earth,
And I will have mercy on *her who had* not obtained mercy;
Then I will say to *those who were* not My people,
'You are My people!'
And they shall say, '*You are* my God!'"

(Hosea 2:23)

All people, from Jews first to Gentiles, will be called the bride of Christ if we believe in Jesus and the saving power that He has declared for us in times past.

That is just a small typology of a minor book of the prophets. At first glance, the books of the prophets can seem harsh and full of judgment, but with context, they reveal the loving-kindness of God for His creation. God is holy, and He wants His people to be set apart, to be in love with Jesus, and to know the true blessings of His people. If riches for all the world came through the rejection of the Israelites not responding to Jesus in faith, how much more will the people of Israel be blessed if they are grafted back into the natural olive branch?

To set an image of Israel's betrayal, God chose to paint a theatrical theme to set an example not only for that generation, but also for the generations after.

The hurt and heartache God has dealt with from the people of Israel over the generations has been astonishing.

The Bible is a love book, but judgments are necessary for His promises of prosperity and peace toward His people so we can receive His truths. Without correction, how can one be corrected?

The Bible can shape our hearts over time, so we can see the love on each page and see an aspect from the heart of God rather than our human thoughts.

As I mentioned before, there is a natural olive branch that is grafted in (see Romans 11:17). The entire world has been endowed to be called the bride of Christ if they will just be willing to believe. Then they will be written into the lamb's Book of Life and be made a treasured people in God's eyes (see Revelation 20:12).

"For I am not ashamed of the gospel of Christ, for it is the power of God to salvation for everyone who believes, for the Jew first and also for the Greek. For in it the righteousness of God is revealed from faith to faith; as it is written, 'The just shall live by faith.'"

(Romans 1:16-17)

"Salvation *has come* to the Gentiles. Now if their fall *is* riches for the world, and their failure riches for the Gentiles, how much more their fullness!"

(Romans 11:11-12)

God has not forgotten His people even though the whole world is now offered a position to be a part of God's royal family. How much more awaits those who are of the seed of Abraham? Their fullness will be with abundance if they return to the Messiah; they then can be grafted in again with belief though faith in Jesus Christ.

God's forgiveness and love is shown there in Romans in that He has not forgotten His people, and the church is not a replacement for the Israelites. There will be a joining of the two into one tree so the fatness will be to the Israelites and then to the world. We can all share in His love as one big family grafted into the tree of grace!!

CHAPTER 12
Royalty Obtained

Let's jump into another book from the prophets, Ezekiel. The book of Ezekiel once again demonstrates God's street theatre to His people and how Israel had again gone astray. Now the Lord is not condescending to them with His theatre, but rather He's trying to gain their attention because they had become hard of hearing.

The Lord had Ezekiel do some odd symbolism to show the people of Israel the judgment He was going to bring upon His people for going astray and worshipping idols of lust and sex and sacrificing newborn babies, which God strongly disapproved of. Israel had become extreme with sins, and the people of Israel had run after foreign gods of other nations. They had forgotten the works of the true and living God who delivered them from their past captivity and trials.

The time is around 600 BC (about 250 years after Hosea had proclaimed the news God wanted to send to His people). The book of Ezekiel can be interpreted in many ways; it is full of symbolism and poetry that can reveal mysteries of the kingdom of God, His holiness, the Holy Temple, and the ark of the covenant. Ezekiel had many visions and tasks God had told him to perform. God had said to him that the people had become hard-hearted toward Him. Even if the prophets of old were to pray for

Israel, He would not listen to the prayers for the people (see Ezekiel 14:14).

Society had become excessively wicked. Israel had never had such an extreme reshuffle from God as what was about to happen. They were to be taken into captivity and under the rule of foreigners and their customs.

Ezekiel proclaimed the Lord's overview: that He would send them into captivity for their sins, but He would take the stony heart from them and give them a heart of flesh (see Ezekiel 36:26).

God was letting Israel know that He was going to take away the idol worship and share the cup of their false gods with them in captivity. But He was also going to give them a way in mercy for the next generations to share an incredible view for His plan of redemption for His people. He declared he was going to give His people His Holy Spirit and to show the love of God poured out in their hearts, so that they could love the Lord and see the treasures that He offers to those who love and obey Him in truth and righteousness.

The book of Ezekiel reveals to us that God had a plan to redeem His people over the long term; to take away the idolatry from His people and to give them His son Jesus Christ; to make a new temple of the Holy Spirit and to be as a fresh stream flowing through His new creation made in Christ (see 2 Corinthians 5:17 and Ezekiel 36:27). God's new holy temple is His believers by the sanctifying work of the Son and the washing of the Word of God.

Again, I want to share some of the love from God through Ezekiel. It's so essential to see the love God has and how He reveals His heart. This Scripture below illustrates the blessing that He had given to Israel when they were struggling and weak. Although there is judgment surrounding the entire book, it's important to see God's view of the love He offered and the rebellion of His people who chose to walk away after receiving His favour.

Ezekiel 16:2-140

"'Thus says the Lord GOD to Jerusalem: "Your birth and your nativity *are* from the land of Canaan; your father *was* an Amorite and your mother a Hittite. *As for* your nativity, on the day you were born your navel cord was not cut, nor were you washed in water to cleanse *you*; you were not rubbed with salt nor wrapped in swaddling cloths. No eye pitied you, to do any of these things for you, to have compassion on you; but you were thrown out into the open field, when you yourself were loathed on the day you were born.

"And when I passed by you and saw you struggling in your own blood, I said to you in your blood, 'Live!' Yes, I said to you in your blood, 'Live!' I made you thrive like a plant in the field; and you grew, matured, and became very beautiful. *Your* breasts were formed, your hair grew, but you *were* naked and bare.

"When I passed by you again and looked upon you, indeed your time *was* the time of love; so I spread My wing over you and covered your nakedness. Yes,

I swore an oath to you and entered into a covenant with you, and you became Mine," says the Lord GOD.

"Then I washed you in water; yes, I thoroughly washed off your blood, and I anointed you with oil. I clothed you in embroidered cloth and gave you sandals of badger skin; I clothed you with fine linen and covered you with silk. I adorned you with ornaments, put bracelets on your wrists, and a chain on your neck. And I put a jewel in your nose, earrings in your ears, and a beautiful crown on your head. Thus you were adorned with gold and silver, and your clothing *was of* fine linen, silk, and embroidered cloth. You ate *pastry of* fine flour, honey, and oil. You were exceedingly beautiful, and succeeded to royalty. Your fame went out among the nations because of your beauty, for it *was* perfect through My splendor which I had bestowed on you," says the Lord GOD.'"

From the very heart of God, His character and loyalty—wow!

What a love story to the most incredible depth of engagement. A people who were abandoned and left to die in the wilderness, but as Ezekiel describes, God found them, nurtured them, and then betrothed them in loving kindness. God's poetry of excellence expounds to us His love for them.

As if they were left to die in the wilderness, as was the custom in that time of some who did not want a child, they were rejected and despised. God found them in blood and said to them, "Live!" In the brokenness and abandonment of people regarded as worthless to the world, God found and made them to live and to become royalty. They obtained riches and mercy by His tender kindness.

The emphasis on this text is to share the heart of God. It shows the care He has and how He wrapped them in His wings of love as a young man cares for his bride-to-be. He made her royalty and gifts of jewels overflowed from her midst. He gave her the most refined items one could ask for: a diamond for her nose, pierced ears, fine linen and silk. These are the most delicate objects fit for a bride-to-be.

To obtain royalty from the dregs of blood and abandonment, the Lord's favour fed her with the best products of the land that had her in high regard. Her prosperity was well known in the world. A people of wealth and splendour, all of which came from the Lord's hand. He patiently waited for the maturity of His people to become the heirs of the king's inheritance. But once again, with the fallen nature, they turned from their God who blessed them with all the goods and turned to harlotry. It goes to say regardless of who the Israelites are, it reveals the human condition of sin in the fallen nature. It reveals why He had to give humans a new heart to be able to share in His riches and favour without falling away. If God had chosen another tribe, the human condition would have still been the same way.

We see the Lord has been eager with tender mercies to reveal himself to His bride. As we know the love of the Lord and the mystery revealed from the gospel, and the love is bestowed upon His church, the people of Israel have to be caught up in love to have the veil removed to enter into the age of grace in order for the fulness of the gentiles to become a part of the adorned royalty belief. A new heart results in finding the riches of salvation and eternal life. We see the Bible declares a covenant marriage proposal to all who are willing as we see in Matthew.

> "'The kingdom of heaven is like a certain king who arranged a marriage for his son, and sent out his servants to call those who were invited to the wedding; and they were not willing to come.'"
>
> (Matthew 22:1-3)

Many are invited who are called, but not everyone wants to listen to the riches and mercy of the love of Christ. Those who are chosen are His people, and they respond to the message of the wedding invitation and become a part of the family of God. There is a typology of the Lord's hand and the marriage of the new covenant revealed from the Old Testament prophets and New Testament apostles.

The Bible talks about how God is full of faithfulness and unfailing love. He lavishes unfailing love toward us to thousands of generations; He gives chances to many and forgives the sins of thousands of generations (see Exodus 34:6-7,1 John 1:9). But ultimately, if at the end of the wicked human condition called sin, the cure (Christ) is rejected and His free gift of love is denied, then there is a rejection that God will declare upon people. The blessings are removed and replaced with curses.

CHAPTER 13

A Vision of a Bride

A little while ago, the Lord gave me a vision. An interesting and unexpected vision, as the Lord usually works that way. He showed me a beautiful ballroom from a bird's eye view, and within the ballroom, I saw a bride with a long white embroidered dress with a wonderfully long train. The bride was swirling around, and the next part shown was Jesus Christ coming in the air to meet His bride. It was fantastic to see the love He had and how His hands were outstretched, and He saw her with a big smile on His face. He was there to greet her with love and to reveal heaven's plans to her.

Now when I refer to "her," it's not that we are in a literal sense a bride as we may understand with our carnality, but rather it's an idiom He uses to show that our relationship with Jesus is like a sacred marriage and it's a bond of love. We are betrothed to Him. So we enter into a covenant of peace and to inherit royalty. Often the Bible shares that believers are abiding in His body, meaning they are under His protection and Christ is the head of us. Once again, it's an idiom to symbolise His unity of one man—the new man made into Christ's image versus the old man, Adam, the sinful nature.

There is another vision that the Lord has given me that I also want to share. It meshes well with the last vision.

He often reveals a glimpse of His heart to me, and how He does it is often very beautiful. This time He showed me a bride standing with a veil on her face. It was a white veil. He then approached the bride and lifted off her veil. This was symbolic of His bride coming to the knowledge of Christ.

"But their minds were blinded. For until this day the
same veil remains unlifted in the reading of the Old
Testament, because the *veil* is taken away in Christ.
But even to this day, when Moses is read, a veil lies
on their heart. Nevertheless when one turns to the Lord,
the veil is taken away. Now the Lord is the Spirit;
and where the Spirit of the Lord *is*, there *is* liberty."

(2 Corinthians 3:14-17)

This is where we have found ourselves in the last two thousand years after Christ died and rose again. The gospel has been preached to the world, and the Word of the Lord is being fulfilled each day. The grace toward the gentiles is open and welcoming to all who wish to enter into the new covenant. The bride is made up of all those who are in Christ's grace and are entering into the kingdom of God through belief.

We see that the apostle Paul talks about how the veil is covering those who do not believe. Unbelief hides the truth; people cannot see the full scope of grace because of the veil, their unbelief. Just as the people of Israel couldn't look at Moses unless the veil was covering his face because of the glory of God, if people turn to the Messiah, Jesus Christ, He lifts off the veil that covers their hearts. We are in exciting times and Jesus is eager to reveal His love again after the diaspora of the Jewish people. Scripture shares the gospel is first for the Israelites and then to the rest of the world.

"For I am not ashamed of the gospel of Christ, for it is the power of God to salvation for everyone who believes, for the Jew first and also for the Greek. For in it, the righteousness of

God is revealed from faith to faith; as it is written,
'The just shall live by faith.'"

(Romans 1:16-17)

The term Greek in those times was a generalised saying for the world because of the empires that had established the world's cultures and languages.

We are coming into a time that will be perilous times, I believe the Lord shared with me, but the Lord is ready to give great grace to His churches around the world for the end-time harvest for souls. We are on our journey to go from faith to faith, and to live by faith to see Christ revealed in glory, like Moses and the Israelites saw the glory of the Lord in times of old.

The Lord also revealed a large harvest field to me, and the harvest was ripe and ready. He said to me with a bold proclamation, "Harvest time!" meaning the kingdom of heaven is ready to reap the world's souls, ready for the return of the king. The bride of Christ is to make herself ready.

"'The marriage of the Lamb has come, and His wife
has made herself ready.' And to her, it was granted to be
arrayed in fine linen, clean and bright, for the fine
linen is the righteous acts of the saints."

(Revelation 19:7-8)

We see in Revelation that Christ is ready to return for His saints. The righteous acts of the saints are their fine linen, and they are holy and prepared for Christ's return. They do good works that lead people to know the glory of God for salvations.

"'Come, I will show you the bride,
the Lamb's wife.'"

(Revelation 21:9)

Here Scripture is referring to the saints as His bride showing us the lamb's wife (believers) and the lamb (Christ), although this end-time harvest could span many years. It's essential to see the symbolic nature of Christ's love for His people (see Ephesians 5:25-27). He wants us to act and respond in faith to His righteous request of showing and sharing His message to the world, inviting all from the highways to the byways so they are ready for the celebration of eternal security for the consecrated marriage.

CHAPTER 14

Happily Forever After

Have you ever wondered why in movies when the wedding cars head off to their destinations, it resembles "a happily forever after" as if the wedding consecrated a perfect world of happiness and joy? But in the stark reality of this world, happily ever after never seems to prosper forever. After all, life is temporary, people can change, and the vastness of time ticks steadily towards decay. But God says in His Word:

> "For I *am* the LORD,
> I do not change."
>
> (Malachi 3:6)

God does not change: it's a comforting thought, isn't it? One who is faithful and is deeply in love with us, one who wants an intimate relationship to share with us details of who He and what he stands for He is one who won't change. He has endless qualities to teach us if we draw near. He is for us, and wants to protect us, and have us be as heirs in His family of love. The Bible says God is love (see 1 John 4:16). We do not honestly know what true love is until we come into the family of God.

In His family, we find a place where we will be accepted and will inherit a home where no one will steal from us or kill us. It's a place where paradise is a reality, where perfect harmony dwells and there is love, peace, joy, prosperity, family, music, and life. There is no death, no pain, no destruction; it's a reality that is out of time, a place called home forever. There is no sin, jealousy, or deceit. It's a place where God makes us secure, and we can build and lay claim to what is truly ours. There, God prepares mansions with our names etched into the wall. The end results in a final destination of peace, where we are ready to learn of the greater microcosms of the extended reality of heaven.

One warm afternoon near a gentle river, I was admiring God's creation. I spoke to the Lord about this world and how large it is. How grand are the universe and the stars? I was in awe at His skills to design the smooth trees and the flickering from the sun on the water, and how this world is floating as only a mere speck in the universe's blanket of creativity.

The Lord spoke to me and said to me that this universe, the world, the creation that we are aware of, is just a microcosm of what He has created for us. I quickly searched for the meaning of microcosm, and my mind was blown. I love the vast array of words God can use to speak to us and how God can use Google to explain words and help me understand meanings that I had never learned of before.

A microcosm is "a community, place, or situation regarded as encapsulating in miniature the characteristics of something much larger," according to Oxford Languages, accessed through Google search.

"Characteristics of something much larger" stands out to me. In this world, we can see the realities of God, as we covered at the start of the book, with His hand in creation. The Bible talks about how this world is just a type of things to come as in celebrations and festivals (see Colossians 2:16). This world is just temporary, and the most fantastic expanse is the reality out of time, the actual creation that is in heaven, the permanent stance of truth with no fabric that could be broken.

That is why we are so lucky to have a second chance in this world. Once we die, we enter into the spirit realm that meets God; God is spirit (see John 4:24). It is a glorified state, and we are either made right with God by His Son, or we are judged by not being found in God's olive tree of grace that allows us to eat from the tree of life (see Revelation 22:1-2). God cannot change because He is not in time. Scientists are now discovering that time is warped, and at the speed of light, there is no time. The Bible declares God is light (see 1 John 1:5). Since God is timeless, the greater reality is in Him, not in our winding down of time and decay of the thermodynamics in this universe that sin allowed death to enter. As the bride of Christ, we will be made in His image as He is glorified; we will also be glorified sinless and holy, joined to be a part of the greater reality that is connected directly to God.

"The Savior, the Lord Jesus Christ, ... will transform our lowly body that it may be conformed to His glorious body, according to the working by which He is able even to subdue all things to Himself."

(Philippians 3:20-21)

As a part of being made perfect, we will be made perfect in His image when we are glorified with Jesus Christ at the end of the age. A trustworthy happily ever after will be achieved there by removing sin and lies. We will be taught by God's grace and see the Father face to face. We will be His adopted children, able to call Him "abba," which means father in Aramaic language (see Romans 8:15)

When the apostle John was full of good old age, he received the book of Revelation in an open vision Jesus gave him while he was on the small island of Patmos. The revelation gave answers to the church and showed what was to come over the last age of grace.

John saw New Jerusalem come down and the judgment of Satan and his angels. He saw all liars and false prophets judged and thrown into the fiery lake for eternity. We see the complexities of the books of the prophets being unwrapped and the scrolls being declared by angels who are ordained to unleash these declarations for the world. These include the removal of sin by faith in Christ and promises to those who overcome the evil one. Those who do overcome will have access to the tree of life. The divine appointment for the kingdom of heaven will take place, our eternal roles will be allocated for the eternal callings, and we will be rewarded with crowns of gold that do not perish!

Revelation tells us the truth that lies ahead. The prophets' proclamations will be unlocked, Scriptures will be fully fulfilled, and God's righteous judgment will deal with unrepentant sinners, while there are rewards for all of His saints.

There will be a city for "the apple of His eye," His people of old all in one family. The father of nations, Abraham, and the spiritual seed of Christ will be joined together, merged, and entwined like a natural olive tree and a wild one grafted in. John reveals the foundations of God's forgiveness: clear, radiant, gold streets; colourful gemstones; and layers of riches. There is a description of the gates and the twelve tribes of Israel will be etched into the city of angels, where a deep, rich history was formed and where His name, the faithful and true one, will reign.

"Then I, John, saw the holy city, New Jerusalem, coming down out of heaven from God, prepared as a bride adorned for her husband. And I heard a loud voice from heaven saying, 'Behold, the tabernacle of God *is* with men, and He will dwell with them, and they shall be His people. God Himself will be with them *and be* their God. And God will wipe away every tear from their eyes; there shall be no more death, nor sorrow, nor crying. There shall be no more pain, for the former things have passed away.'"

(Revelation 21:2-4)

There will be a new world created in love, overflowing with peace and joy. All pain will be gone, and former things will no longer be remembered. There will be a happily ever after and a faithful and true word given to us by the Lord, a holy promise sealed with His covenant that He has given to His bride-to-be.

After the fallen world of sin is done and the devil and his demons are thrown into hell for eternity, there will be the great white throne of judgment. All those who have sinned and are not found in the book of life will be revealed. All secrets will be opened wide for all of creation to see.

There will be an eternal judgment for what has been done on that righteous, holy day for all wrongs in this universe to be made right with God's holy wisdom, and final say!

Oh, what a day that will be! When injustices are met with a just reward, and judgment on demons and humans who have caused pain and sinned against God is passed.

Have you ever been asked the question, If you were to remove one thing from the world, what would it be? I hear people sometimes say greed, some others hate, some say cancer or pain. Many people have a correct view on these subjects, but they often overlook the most critical issue: sin. If sin was removed from the world, what would exist? Righteousness and peace. No evil. Removing sin is the key to eliminating all other issues in life.

The core foundation of this fallen world is a result of sin and curses from rebellion and not being in harmony with our holy God. Jesus Christ is the answer to the removal of sin; He alone is the only cure. We can get a glimpse in Revelation of what our new world will look like without sin. There will be no more world issues of hunger, greed, hatred, division, or disease, but true world peace will exist.

Jesus will reign in truth and in love; harmony will be upon those who love Him. A world of blessing is described as pure gold streets. Gold is so pure, it is like glass! We will be in the midst of God and His angels and living with Him, sharing a pristine, crystal-clear river of life flowing from the heart of God. It will go through the middle of the city, leading to the tree of life, and healing will be in its leaves! Death will no longer have dominion over life. The new world will be free from sin and lies; even though it has been hard living in a fallen world, we will know what true blessing we have found in the paradise of God, who is tested, tried, and holy. We will be pure to see God's face and ready to live and to learn of His goodness. If that sounds wonderful, let's explore in the next chapter how Jesus is the captain of our souls who leads us safely to our new destination, but let's finish this chapter with a true happily ever after with the Word of the Lord.

Revelation 21:18-27

"The construction of its wall was *of* jasper; and the city *was* pure gold, like clear glass. The foundations of the wall of the city *were* adorned with all kinds of precious stones: the first foundation *was* jasper, the second sapphire, the third chalcedony, the fourth emerald, the fifth sardonyx, the sixth sardius, the seventh chrysolite, the eighth beryl, the ninth topaz, the tenth chrysoprase, the eleventh jacinth, and the twelfth amethyst. The twelve gates *were* twelve pearls: each individual gate was of one pearl. And the street of the city *was* pure gold, like transparent glass.

"But I saw no temple in it, for the Lord God Almighty and the Lamb are its temple. The city had no need of the sun or of the moon to shine in it, for the glory of God illuminated it. The Lamb *is* its light. And the nations of those who are saved shall walk in its light, and the kings of the earth bring their glory and honor into it. Its gates shall not be shut at all by day (there shall be no night there). And they shall bring the glory and the honor of the nations into it. But there shall by no means enter it anything that defiles, or causes an abomination or a lie, but only those who are written in the Lamb's Book of Life."

CHAPTER 15

The Captain of Our Souls

Jesus is our destined leader. Hebrews tells us that Jesus is the captain of our salvation (see Hebrews 2:10). There is comfort in knowing we have a leader who can understand what we go through in this life. Jesus Himself was tempted in many areas, but He did not sin. Hebrews talks about how we have a high priest who can sympathise with us (see Hebrews 4:15).

We have Jesus to lead us and access to the throne of grace through what He has done. His actions of love show us how leaders are to be. To be a true leader means serving others and putting others' needs above your own. That's precisely what Jesus did. Jesus showed us by teaching His disciples to help one another. That is what the kingdom of heaven is all about. Each person should esteem others higher than themselves (see Philippians 2:3). To always be learning and leaning on Jesus is to have humility and to be teachable in the correct ways of love.

"'Come to Me, all *you* who labor and are heavily laden,
and I will give you rest. Take My yoke upon you and
learn from Me, for I am gentle and lowly in heart,
and you will find rest for your souls.
For My yoke *is* easy, and My burden is light.'"

(Matthew 11:28-30)

Do you want to find rest for your souls? Jesus states clearly that He will give us rest if we take His yoke, His will, His love to share and that we are to learn from Him. He says He is gentle and quiet in heart. We can take refuge in One who is faithful and seeks out the hurt and crushed. He cares and is willing to go to great lengths to save one who is lost.

> "'What man of you, having a hundred sheep, if he loses one of them, does not leave the ninety-nine in the wilderness, and go after the one which is lost until he finds it? And when he has found *it*, he lays *it* on his shoulders, rejoicing. And when he comes home, he calls together *his* friends and neighbors, saying to them, "Rejoice with me, for I have found my sheep which was lost!" I say to you that likewise there will be more joy in heaven over one sinner who repents than over ninety-nine just persons who need no repentance.'"
>
> (Luke 15:4-7)

In the parable of the lost sheep, Jesus shares the great effort one would go to, to find a sheep that's lost and bring it back into the fold under the shepherd's protection. Christ finds those who are lost, and He carries them back Himself with rejoicing. There are many celebrations in heaven: as the parable shared, when one sinner repents and is turned to righteousness, all of heaven rejoices! What love that all of heaven rejoices at the sight of one who was lost being found and saved. That shepherd is our captain, champion, and the victor that leads our faith.

As our captain, He is full of mercy. Many people often feel that they cannot be forgiven for their past sins. First, I want to share with you how our captain, Jesus, understands exactly what sin is and He understood what He did for us on the cross. Sometimes the devil can try to plant seeds of discouragement, maybe saying, "You cannot be forgiven" or "You will fail" or "This time you've mucked up and God won't accept you this time."

The devil can try to discourage us, and if he achieves that, we can tend to say why bother trying anymore? Sometimes we fall back into the ways of sin and become hardened toward God. This approach is not from God, and this condemnation is not God's heart toward us. Jesus was asked, if one sins against another, how many times should they be forgiven? Jesus said seventy times seven! (See Matthew 18:21-22). Basically, Jesus was saying always forgive, and a true repentance will always be accepted before God. If we come before Him and ask for mercy, He has determined in His heart to bless us with grace (see Zechariah 8:14-17).

When Jesus was with His disciples teaching the multitudes at the temple, some religious leaders tried to trap Jesus with all their laws and customs they upheld with their own righteousness. They were not able to discern God's grace. They threw a lady who was caught in the act of adultery before Jesus's feet. They wanted Jesus to judge her according to the law of Moses. They understood that Jesus was compassionate toward people, and they understood that God's law could not be contradicted. They wanted to trap Jesus in going against the law of God. But little did they know that God was bringing in a new law: a law of love, a law of mercy and peace toward His people. Grace was to be shown. Rather than the law of Moses that aroused death,

Christ was bringing forth grace that gave forgiveness unto righteousness. Something the self-righteous Pharisees were blinded to.

> "'He who is without sin among you,
> let him throw a stone at her first.'"
> (John 8:7)

Jesus basically said, "Who can judge you? Who can throw the first stone?" No one dared throw the first stone because all understood they had sinned. The Pharisees slowly dissipated, with the elders leaving first, because Jesus taught wisdom. The only person who could have bent down and picked up a rock was Jesus! But He chose to offer forgiveness. This is the grace that Jesus offers to us when we sin. He forgives us and teaches us the right path to be the captain of our souls.

"'Where are your accusers? Didn't even one of them condemn you?'

"'No, Lord,' she said.

> "And Jesus said, 'Neither do I. Go and sin no more.'"
> (John 8:10-11 NLT)

> "'I am the light of the world. If you follow me, you won't
> have to walk in darkness, because you will have the light
> that leads to life.'"
> (John 8:12 NLT)

Jesus is teaching that if we sin, we should ask for forgiveness and move on toward His ways that bring forth life. He does not condemn us if we fail. We have His grace, and Christ's offering atones for us. Sin no more, He said; He does not advocate for us to sin and get away with it. Rather, He wants us to learn from our paths for sincere faith toward Him. Much that is forgiven results in a greater love because we experience His latitude of mercies and grace (see Luke 7:47). If we are following the captain of our souls, He rejoices to see us on the right path, and if we are sincere in asking forgiveness, we will love Him so much more because of His tender mercies He reveals in our lives. We will have the light that reveals to us that walking in darkness is painful and foolish. We know that the light, who is Christ, leads us to eternal life.

CHAPTER 16

The Author of Our Paths

When my wife was a young girl, she knew that she was going to marry a man from a small town that her grandparents lived in. She was from Melbourne, one of the larger cities in Australia, and this small town was about two hours from Melbourne. She and her family were not Christian, yet Jesus had laid upon her heart this knowledge of her husband-to-be: me! You see, Jesus starts writing chapters of our life before we can even come to know Him. The knowledge God can place within our hearts that directs and guides us is simply amazing.

When I was about 13 years old, my parents ran a church in Melbourne, even though we lived in that small town near where her grandparents lived. Through going to Melbourne for church, I was familiar with the city. I loved to skateboard all around Melbourne when we went up there on the weekends. Being a young teenager who loved the thrill of skateboarding, I would ask my parents if I could go the city's central skatepark, which soon became my weekend home, I went there after the morning church service.

I often wanted to skateboard and enjoy time with my friends in the city. My parents did not force me to go to church but gave me the option. In all that time, God was working my life out for good. With the good and bad experiences of city living I became more street smart, and

God taught me some major life lessons, but as kids we all get up to mischief and we learn from the journeys we take. God is amazing, when I look back, I can see His hand guiding my life when I was not aware of Him. He shapes and moulds us for His plans to reveal Christ love through us and His wisdom, when we are ready to respond. He can merge people's paths and interconnect relationships before we are even aware!

One day, I was invited to a birthday party in the city, and as a young kid looking to meet new people and have some fun, I went to this party. Funny enough, while at the party, I met my wife-to-be when I was thirteen years old. We began talking, and she asked where I was from. I said, "Oh, well, you won't know this place; I'm from a small country town in the middle of nowhere." Then she said, "Oh, I may know," with a small inquisitive grin on her face. I stated the town, and she later told me she laughed inside to herself.

At that time, I was not interested in dating her back then (call me stupid), but I pursued her friend instead, which quickly did not amount to much at that age. But God had introduced us; what Jesus had revealed to her when she was very young was now unfolding. She also liked me a lot at the time; she said to God, "If you're real, God, you will bring him to me," after I showed interest for her friend instead.

She was quite demanding, and I had to laugh after I heard it, but ... with a smile, God must have had the last laugh, as He probably thought to Himself; hook line and sinker, the connection has been made! God kept our groups of friends close, and we all associated with similar people.

We mostly went to the same gatherings for about three to four years, but oddly, we never really ran into each other. I often think back at how God had His hand upon us both, and how He had His timing for us to meet again, possibly when I had matured a little more … He had written that chapter for our lives to merge, and so it did!

We ended up meeting again and fully chatting—finally—when we were sixteen, and we have been together since. It's interesting to see how Jesus can guide our lives for good and to be a part of His plan. Shortly after meeting her, I shared the gospel with her, even though I was lukewarm and still did not attend church. God was writing our chapters and being the author of our faith. Ultimately, He was leading us to His love to know His realities and eventually to joining the ministry much later down the road.

It's amazing to see how God had planted the knowledge within my wife's heart at a young age and how He guides and shares His heart with us. Even though for quite a while after meeting her, I was on my own path away from Jesus, my wife began to support and help me in my life. She had a godly wisdom that I did not have at the time. She guided me out of trouble. She was longsuffering and patient with my unwillingness to grow up. She supported me and trusted that God would guide me into His love.

I was walking away from Christ. I was on my own path of destruction. I had gone through some significant health scares with about eighty-five blood clots, called pulmonary embolism, that nearly took me out; the doctors were amazed I was still standing. But God had a plan.

Jesus showed me His love in an extraordinary way, to say the least. I was sitting on my bed, and Jesus gave me an open vision. An open vision is different than seeing a picture in the mind's eye; it's as if I was literally there in person and experiencing what was in front of me.

Jesus showed me His face, a perfect face, made up of stars, excellent and full of love with His presence flowing over my body. Then the star of His face, which made up His characteristics, quickly dispersed out to space, vast and wondrous. Then Jesus took me in the spirit to New York's Central Park. It was fall, the leaves were falling, and people were walking in snow jackets and beanies. It was so vivid and with a purpose that only God knows, but then I came back to sitting on my bed in shock and amazement. I did not know what I had just experienced. I kept this to myself for some time.

Jesus made Himself real to me, and maybe I was a hard nut to crack, but He showed me His love, and boy, I am glad I know Him. He is a wonderful saviour, and how He leads us is simply by His grace and love. God has many ways of intercepting us and using His hand to bring the best out of us. He knows how to equip us and encourage us for times that lay ahead. He truly is the author of our faith, and if we keep our eyes upon Him, God works all things out for good.

If we look at the Bible verse we covered in the previous chapter about Jesus giving us rest, He says learn of me. That's precisely what God wants all of His children to do. We have the entire Bible that leads us to His truths and reveals His love and allows us to know Him intimately.

Shortly after the open vision, He told me to "study up," using the modern slang I was accustomed to. I was amazed when He spoke to me and told me to learn of His ways. His voice is full of love; it's colourful, and each word has meaning and care behind it. When He said my name, Joel, it was as if each letter lit up with vivid colours of love in His speech. It's simply amazing that His speech is somehow colourful and loving; it's like a supernatural, multifaceted voice with power!

That is the captain we serve. He wants all of us to know Him and to learn of His ways. Often when growing up, I would think to myself, "I don't need the Bible," for whatever reason; I was blinded by pride or wanting to know things that instead puffed up the flesh and things that did not result in godly fruit, but I was significantly mistaken. I have received such wealth and knowledge by learning of God and His ways. It's a walk; I will always be studying and learning from Jesus. Part of discipleship is to be improving and to be learning to love as He does.

God's Word is there to direct our steps; His Word is to light our path as we walk in faith (see Psalm 37:23, Psalm 119:105)

How will we know what to do if we are not in the Bible? How are we to gain godly wisdom if we are not learning of His ways? God's Word teaches us prudence, diligence, and foundational integrity. When we allow the Word of God in our hearts, we can then grow with the Lord and allow Him to disciple us.

Just as Jesus walked with the twelve disciples, He also wants to walk with us. First, He will let us know who He is. Then, He will explain the way things are and what is to come. Then Jesus's love and truth can prepare our hearts for growth to be established in His ways.

A lot of Christians can struggle with hearing the Holy Spirit's voice, but He still talks to us. Just because Jesus has come and fulfilled the cross does not mean He no longer speaks. He does speak to us every day. It's not always vivid and audible— it's very rare that happens—but often it can be knowledge placed within our hearts, and it's a matter of discerning the things of His Spirit.

Since we have His Holy Spirit, it's even more of a reason for us to be closer to God because of His Son! What helps us to learn to hear His voice is knowing His ways. If we know who He is, we can gain trust and He can give us more understanding that leads to a greater responsibility. It's not that He needs to trust us, but rather we can allow the Holy Spirit in our lives more, so we do not hurt ourselves by ignoring His paths.

Jesus wants each of His followers to be walking out the calling He has given them, and knowing His voice can be challenging. We need to remember that we are spiritual beings. We are renewed, and our inner man is spiritual. To hear God's voice is an essential aspect of following Jesus and being guided in His paths.

As we become humble and are open to God's truths, we can then start to develop the inner man by allowing the mind of Christ to reveal to us His love. As we have senses— taste, touch, etc—our spirit man also has senses. For example, have you ever been in a car and randomly looked around because you sensed someone looking at you? How did you know that? There's no logical way, is there?

We are integrated with more than just our carnal senses; we are spiritual. God usually uses our spiritual senses to speak to us by our spirit man. This can happen by allowing the Word of God to feed our inner man. We can then start to learn of His ways, become more sensitised to the realm of the spirit, and be in tune with our renewed spirit man so we can hear God's voice. I'm lucky to have had a few encounters with the Lord to direct me to His truths; grace has certainly been working within my life. That has enabled me to be able to share my experiences with learning God's ways.

The Western world can sometimes be numb toward the spiritual. There are many people around the world who are aware of their spirituality, but often it's not of God. But He created us with soul, spirit, and body. God uses these means for His Christians to be spiritual too! The devil is an imitator and tries to create a taboo in the Christian world by suggesting being spiritual is bad. It is bad if you are spiritual without Christ, but if we are guided with His Holy Spirit and empowered by Jesus, it is the communion Christ purchased for us! We are to be like Christ! To be His disciples is to be spiritual and moving in the supernatural for His glory.

God does not want carnal Christians who have unbelief of spiritual giftings. He wants us trained and ready to fight the good fight of faith; we wrestle not with flesh and blood but evil spirits (see Ephesians 6:12). We have the Holy Spirit, and if we believe, we are in communion with the Holy Spirit. It is our right as children of God to hear His voice and His leadings and be active in our spiritual armour to fight for truth. We are not to be seat warmers, but His ministers: a flame of fire, to be trained and believing in the spiritual rights He has given us.

God communicates in many ways, and as disciples, it is a faith walk, but Jesus says in John 10:27-28:

"My sheep hear My voice, and I know them, and they follow Me. And I give them eternal life, and they shall never perish; neither shall anyone snatch them out of My hand."

The key word here is as we follow Jesus, we will learn how He talks to us. We are all different and unique, but we do need to exercise our spiritual growth and help it be nurtured for discipleship. For example, if I were to work out in a gym, I would feed my muscles before a workout and after, right? So, we need to give our spirit man the spiritual food to grow in our walk with Jesus. That food is knowing His ways, learning humility, showing love, and being sensitive to the Holy Spirit and the giftings He has given us by exercising our faith so we can grow.

"Therefore I remind you to stir up the gift of God
which is in you through the laying on of my hands.
For God has not given us a spirit of fear, but of
power and of love and of a sound mind."

(2 Timothy 1:6-7)

As part of Jesus being the author of our paths, often Christ will lead us to step out and to use our faith, to hear God's voice and be aware of His leadings so we can serve Him in a spiritual sense. To be Christian soldiers is to be skilfully trained by Jesus to discern good and evil and to fight for the truth with Him leading us. Building our relationship with the Holy Spirit is so essential to hearing His voice and then accepting His directions by faith.

The Holy Spirit is often referred to as a dove, and doves are usually very gentle, and they are easily scared. I'm not saying that the Holy Spirit is ever scared, but we are to be in an environment that welcomes His presence. If we are walking in love, we will not be neglecting His ways and it will enhance our sensitivity to the Holy Spirit in our journey. Walking in the Holy Spirit will enable us to be connected to Him, and we will have a rapport with His will in our lives. Worshipping Jesus out of pure and honest hearts is precious before God, and blessing will follow as we will cover below!

Jesus shares about the qualities He is looking for in the beatitudes. Beatitudes mean "blessedness" to those who are very blessed. When He shares the beatitudes, Jesus is teaching His disciples and the multitudes. He is revealing the children of God's best characteristics so He can bless them. He shares even if we are going through hard times with persecutions in this life, we are blessed because of His grace toward us. Jesus is teaching from His heart to the people to show these qualities, and if we follow them, it will result in us being supremely blessed.

"'Blessed *are* the poor in spirit,
For theirs is the kingdom of heaven.
Blessed *are* those who mourn,
For they shall be comforted.
Blessed *are* the meek,
For they shall inherit the earth.

Blessed *are* those who hunger and
thirst for righteousness,
For they shall be filled.
Blessed *are* the merciful,
For they shall obtain mercy.
Blessed *are* the pure in heart,
For they shall see God.
Blessed *are* the peacemakers,
For they shall be called sons of God.
Blessed *are* those who are persecuted
for righteousness' sake,
For theirs is the kingdom of heaven.

"'Blessed are you when they revile and persecute you, and say all kinds of evil against you falsely for My sake. Rejoice and be exceedingly glad, for great *is* your reward in heaven, for so they persecuted the prophets who were before you.'"

(Matthew 5:3-12)

Jesus is teaching us that even if He is directing our paths, we will still run into issues in life. The true gospel is not always prosperity, as some try to share, but suffering, patience, and truth. Jesus is the captain of our salvation, and in sufferings, He leads us to perfection.

"For it was fitting for him, for whom *are* all things and by whom *are* all things, in bringing many sons to glory, to make the captain of their salvation perfect **through sufferings**."

(Hebrews 2:10, emphasis added)

There can be false perspectives in some modern Christian theology about what life should look like, that you will become blessed and prosperous. The last three words are valid, but maybe not in this life. God can make us prosper, but usually His kingdom blessings are for the eternal rewards; it's not always depicting prosperity on earth. The Bible is very clear about Christians being persecuted for their faith and overcoming. If we look at most of the apostles, they suffered beatings, stonings, ridicule, shame, and separation from loved ones, and most were brutally killed and became martyrs.

Look at what Jesus went through on the cross. His Word has been clear, but people twist sound Scriptures (see 2 Peter 3:14-18) to promote a lifestyle of being blessed rather than walking out the qualities of the beatitudes. People can miss the entire meaning of what the Bible is teaching, and false teachers can lead many astray for greed and wrong motives.

"Preach the word! Be ready in season *and* out of season. Convince, rebuke, exhort, with all longsuffering and teaching. For the time will come when they will not endure sound doctrine, but according to their own desires, *because* they have itching ears, they will heap up for themselves teachers; and they will turn *their* ears away from the truth, and be turned aside to fables. But you be watchful in all things, **endure afflictions**, do the work of an evangelist, fulfill your ministry."

(2 Timothy 4:2-5, emphasis added)

To learn God's voice, we must have a good heart ready for the truth. If we know the truth, but reject it, it could be worse for us in the long term. Jesus wants our hearts to be glad and prepared to accept His teachings and words, so we can act on them and the door can be opened to us as we are diligent to seek Him.

"Be diligent to present yourself approved to God,
a worker who does not need to be ashamed,
rightly dividing the word of truth."
(2 Timothy 2:15)

It's so essential to rightly divide the Word of God. Many people want to lean on other people's understandings of the Scriptures. It can be terrific to learn from others, but if you follow someone too closely and they fall, you will also. Be careful always to be following Jesus first, your heart (your inner witness), then with thoughtful prayer what others are teaching. God will not contradict Himself, and to read the Bible verses with correct context will lead us on the correct path.

I've watched many preachers on major networks quote the Bible and completely bypass Jesus's meaning and twist Scriptures toward their agenda. It's so wrong to try and stretch the Word of God into ways that try to make the Father's house a place to profit, and it can become integrated into their teachings for donations that results in blessings and to sell their products when Jesus should be the focus. There shouldn't be marketing to sell Christians products for self-gain, but rather for edification and to help to the body of Christ (see John 2:16). Now God is the judge on what are the motives of the heart, but when product times exceed salvation messages and prayer for unity, then there is a problem.

Many people can be led astray by some teachings that can result in a fruitless walk and a lack of understanding in their discipleship. It can result in frustration and being taught the incorrect meanings that will not profit anyone but the leadership. We see in John 2:17 and Psalm 69:9 it says:

"'Zeal for Your house has eaten Me up.'"

Jesus was peace bearing, loving, kind, and graceful toward adulterers, murderers, blasphemers, prostitutes, thieves—well let's say every sin besides a few—and He was in a holy righteous anger, flipping over tables and whipping at people making a profit from people selling birds for sacrifices that would cover sin. It was not aimed at the people buying the birds, but it was anger at the merchants trying to make a profit off God's laws and commandments. There needs to be extra care taken and thoughtfulness in motives, time, and understanding when selling Christian products for gain, and if it's used to help people grow, it is essential, but if it's to make money first, then many people can run into error.

"But those who desire to be rich fall into temptation and a snare, and *into* many foolish and harmful lusts which drown men in destruction and perdition. For the love of money is a root of all *kinds of* evil, for which some have strayed from the faith in their greediness, and pierced themselves through with many sorrows."

(1 Timothy 6:10)

These are eternal rewards and losses the Bible teaches about. By being pulled into the riches of some preacher's false prosperity gospel of a perfected life, you may forfeit your eternal rewards at the judgment seat of God. Jesus wants His disciples to lay down their lives and to pick up their cross daily to share with Christ the cup that He had to drink. There are genuine rewards, but usually they are not prideful things of this earth. It's so profitable to understand these things because keeping a healthy understanding to keep away from lustful greed is success in God's eyes. Unfortunately, many Christians can live seeking and listening to preachers they heap up for themselves as we saw in the Scriptures we covered before, and that can result in a fruitless life and a lack of a relationship with Jesus (by their own doing). Many will have much to answer for when they meet Jesus. There will be lots of Christians who will regret not wanting to serve Him more (see 1 Corinthians 3:15).

"Do not love the world or the things in the world. If anyone loves the world, the love of the Father is not in him. For all that *is* in the world—the lust of the flesh, the lust of the eyes, and the pride of life—is not of the Father but is of the world. And the world is passing away, and the lust of it; but he who does the will of God abides forever."

(1 John 2:15-17)

"Now if anyone builds on this foundation *with* gold, silver, precious stones, wood, hay, straw, each one's work will become clear; for the Day will declare it, because it will be revealed by fire; and the fire will test each one's work, of what sort it is. If anyone's work which he has built on *it* endures, he will receive a reward. If anyone's work is burned, he will suffer loss; but he himself will be saved, yet so as through fire.

> "Do you not know that you are the temple of God
> and *that* the Spirit of God dwells in you? If anyone
> defiles the temple of God, God will destroy him.
> For the temple of God is holy, which *temple* you are."
> (1 Corinthians 3:12-17)

The Bible teaches believers will receive rewards. Our work will be tested to see if it was done with the right motives or not. People can become Christians for the false riches and security in this life. Some Christian communities are superficial and have no roots in love. It's important to know that Jesus will test all who have laboured for Him either honestly or deceitfully.

You may say to me, "Joel, this is quite blunt." I know it is, and I say it with love, but it's what the Bible teaches. There are many hard teachings in the Bible because God wants us to be willing and to understand the cost of discipleship. Many of Jesus's disciples left Him when He taught harder truths:

> "Therefore many of His disciples, when they heard
> *this,* said, 'This is a hard saying; who can understand it?'

> 'When Jesus knew in Himself that His disciples complained
> about this, He said to them, 'Does this offend you?'"
> (John 6:60-61)

He is the author of our paths, He is I AM, and it's up to us if we want to follow His teachings or to walk away. But after many followers left Him, Jesus asked His twelve disciples if they wanted to leave Him as well.

> "But Simon Peter answered Him, 'Lord, to whom shall we go? You have the words of eternal life. Also we have come to believe and know that You are the Christ, the Son of the living God.'"
>
> (John 6:68-69)

They had already given everything up; they had nowhere to go! They had set their hearts on wanting to be His disciples because He holds eternal life! Many of the other disciples who left Him had been following Him only for what He could offer them now: He was feeding the multitudes, the sick were being healed, and many wonders were taking place. But as soon as Jesus shared with them their true spiritual need and gave them spiritual food and teaching for eternal life, it was too hard to deal with, so many were unfaithful and left.

Jesus wants us to be open to His ways as seen in the beatitudes and to love and to follow Him. I believe Jesus rebukes many who are in these false doctrines, and He will bless them if they respond with repentance. God wants believers to have the heart of the beatitudes; when we do, our paths will be directed, and God's Word will not be hidden from the feet of those who have prepared their feet with peace and honesty.

Hearing God's voice can be a journey, and we are all in different stages of our walk. I remember a preacher once saying everyone has different experiences and different callings to fulfil and we all respond in different ways and timings. It's important that we as Christians do not judge others who may be involved in false ideas. Rather, we should pray for them and help guide them away from false ideas over time. We all are in different stages, and to get to the end sometimes requires us to learn from mistakes along the way. The beatitudes teach us that those who hunger and thirst for righteousness will be supremely blessed. Those who hate injustices will thirst for the truth to be shared. We must in love direct people with seeds of grace and reveal the errors of false ideas they may listen to. It's all a journey, but for now, let's quickly get back to my wife's story and how God can birth within us a journey of faith before we even come to the knowledge of Christ!

Just as my wife understood she would marry a man from a small town her grandparents lived in, God spoke to her quietly within her heart about me, and she had that understanding downloaded into her spirit.

That is one of many ways God can speak. For example, I understood I would become a preacher when I was older, yet I did not understand how that would ever happen. I was shy and reserved! God can direct and lead our lives in ways that can make sense to us even if we never expressed or thought logically about them.

God's leadings can grow as we are open to the faith, and as we walk by faith in them, His light shines on our steps.

"The steps of a *good* man are ordered by the LORD,
And He delights in his way.
Though he fall, he shall not be utterly cast down;
For the LORD upholds *him with* His hand."

(Psalm 37:23-24)

God's grace is there to empower us and to equip sons and daughters of the living God. His ways direct us by His grace to show us His love each step of the way.

You may be saying, "Where do I start? How do I learn God's voice and directions?" The best place is to make a start! Eating an elephant starts with one mouthful. God's Word can be a big undertaking, but if you break it down into small sections and learn of His ways over a period of time, a lot can be achieved, and growth can come from that.

Did you know you can listen to the entire Bible in around seventy-two hours? Some people can watch a TV series over a week or two, which can be equivalent to half the Bible! God wants diligence, and the rewards from that can be satisfying. It's good to invest time into our spiritual growth; many people can cultivate other areas in life but overlook the most important one. And that is Jesus Christ. To start learning of Jesus's ways is the wisest thing one could ever do.

Our steps are ordered and learning Jesus's ways will lead us to safety and blessing under God's wings. As we grow in the Scriptures and understand how Jesus wants to form His character within us, we will soon start to change into His image. As a process takes place and as the seeds germinate, we can apply them to our lives and Jesus will be shown from the beatitudes we learn all over the Bible.

When our relationship with Him grows as we walk in faith, He will start to direct us because we are living in His newness of life, our minds will be renewing each day toward His thoughts, and we will be led by His Spirit because we will have the urge to love one another. To be a disciple is to be following Jesus each day and living in His Holy Spirit as a lifestyle overtaken by Christ's character of love. As we yield our lives toward these urges of peace and generosity toward others, Christ will be formed in us, and we will see His blessing within our lives. The Holy Spirit is the richness within our lives to receive His blessings and promises that help us overcome these perilous times.

Learning God's voice is not always a quick process, but it's a process that will direct our paths for His will. Once we start to yield toward God's will for our lives, the Holy Spirit will open His love to guide us. The Holy Spirit is our helper, and He teaches us all the things we need to be His disciples of peace.

"These things I have written to you concerning those who *try to* deceive you. But the anointing which you have received from Him abides in you, and you do not need that anyone teach you; but as the same anointing teaches you concerning all things, and is true, and is not a lie, and just as it has taught you, you will abide in Him."

(1 John 2:26-27)

CHAPTER 17

From God's Eyes and Not Ours

Jesus knows the best in us even if we cannot see it. I remember talking to the Lord one night, and I was, well, let's say politely arguing with an instruction He had asked me to do. I remember saying, "I cannot do it, Lord! I don't know how!!"

But He said to me, "I formed you!" Well, that shut me up! Yes, He did, He formed me. He made me the way He made me!! He knows best. God changed my perspective of myself with those three words "I formed you". "Of course," I thought to myself, "I knew that He created me, but it took His grace to tell me, 'Hey kiddo, I know what I'm doing!' How stupid am I to argue with God?"

He knows us much better than we know ourselves. He understands all our insecurities, our motives, and our desires. It's all open before Him. He knows all the talents and the giftings He has placed within us! He must get a laugh out of us sometimes, possibly with a little frustration. I'm not proud of that, but it taught me that God is such an intimate creator. He knows what we can or cannot do.

There are a few examples from the Bible I want to share about how He sees us. Jesus does things very differently from man's understanding. With humans, we can tend to look on the outside of the person's appearance, rather than the inside or their heart, and you may say,

"Well, that's not possible!" And partly, you are right, but God can reveal to us people's hearts with the Holy Spirit, so what I mean by the inside is their heart, soul, integrity, and the person's character.

Many people give fake fronts and not really be what they often proclaim. People are good at projecting what they are not. Jesus is skilful at using people who are often overlooked by society. He did it with the twelve apostles and many other leaders over the years. It's a theme that God's love is revealed to those who are cast aside, broken, and often hurt. He sees the heart of the person and not the counterfeit fronts people so often reveal to others within their own empowerment.

Even David was overlooked when the prophet Samuel asked his father Jesse to gather all His sons so he could anoint one as the new king of Israel. Jesse left out one son, David; he was the smallest and the youngest of their family! Jesse overlooked him and thought, "Why would God give the smallest, least warrior-like son a prominent leadership role as king of Israel?"

"But the LORD said to Samuel, 'Do not look at his appearance or at his physical stature, because I have refused him. For *the LORD does not* see as man sees; for man looks at the outward appearance, but the LORD looks at the heart.'"

(1 Samuel 16:7)

The prophet Samuel asked Jesse if all his sons were there. And Jesse replied, "All but one who is looking after the sheep." God knows what's within a man or woman's heart. This example should reveal to us as Christians that it's not always the outward appearance, prestige, talents, or age that matters. It's what Jesus sees on the inside that matters: the ripe and ready heart of a leader who loves and is prepared to be humble and to learn of God.

Jesus is concerned with the heart of man, not what we can offer Him for immediate results. This is what makes the best leaders. It's seeing the best in a person regardless of the paradigm of society. The most effective way of getting the best from His people is to choose the suitable soil ready to show love. King David became one of the most feared warriors, perhaps small in stature, but big in heart. We all know the story of David and Goliath and the triumph that surrounded that great victory by faith in God's ability to deliver him.

Jesus saw the best in David even though he was a humble shepherd boy with no claim whatsoever to royalty. God bestowed His blessing and ordained him to become a king, a leader like Christ. He was told that he was a man after God's own heart.

> "'He raised up for them David as king, to whom also He gave testimony and said, "I have found David the *son* of Jesse, a man after My *own* heart, who will do all My will."'"
>
> (Acts 13:22)

King David was a psalmist, leader, battle commander, and a young man! God caused him to become strong and blessed David with His graces and mercies. He gave him the key that opened the door to righteousness through Christ, who was to come from the seed of David. Even though David said to God that he and his house were not worthy (see 2

Samuel 7:18), it shows us God's love to appoint a leader, not by man's ideas and ways, but by the heart and the condition that God sees ready to be moulded into His image.

Let's look at Gideon! What a fantastic event of faith in history he helped lead, inspiring millions. A friend once told me about the story of Gideon and how God saw his timeline as a movie reel played out from start to end. That analogy has always stayed in my mind about his journey of faith. Gideon was a man who at first glance seemed scared and quiet and tried to mind his own business without confrontations. He was a hard worker who was diligent in what he did but was often overlooked. Jesus saw Gideon and called him a mighty man of valour. (It was often understood in those times an angel could also mean "one who was sent." When I refer to the angel of the LORD, it can be Jesus in a theophany, meaning an appearance of God. Sometimes other appearances were by an angel of the Lord, meaning created beings, but many people believe today that Jesus was in fact called the angel of the Lord before He was known to men as Jesus Christ. [10] [11] See Judges 6:22; Judges 13:21,22; Joshua 5:13-15)

---

[10] Don Stewart, "Who Is the Angel of the Lord in the Old Testament?" BlueLetterBible.org, https://www.blueletterbible.org/faq/don_stewart/don_stewart_26.cfm, Aug. 4, 2022.

[11] "Who is the angel of the Lord?" GotQuestions.org, https://www.gotquestions.org/angel-of-the-Lord.html, Aug. 4, 2022.

"The angel of the LORD appeared to him, and said to him,
'The LORD *is* with you, you mighty man of valor!'"

(Judges 6:12)

Gideon must have looked and said, "Who, me...?" The angel of the Lord saw this young man who had the heart of a valiant, mighty warrior. Jesus saw Gideon's timeline play out in the present and future. God understood who He was choosing, and He called out to that warrior inside! "Oh, mighty man of valour!" On the outward appearance, Gideon must have thought, "Oh, you have the wrong person," but Jesus knew Gideon was the man for the job.

Jesus saw his timeline and the ending of who Gideon was to become. Jesus, with patience and love, revealed that He was for him and was on his side to conquer Israel's enemies. At the time, Israel was under heavy bondage from the Midianites because of Israel falling away from God and thus leaving their protection and strength.

God cared for His people, and once again, He sent a deliverer into the camps of Israel. This man was Gideon. He was to pull down the false god of Baal and to rise with an army ready to fight and to take back their land. But this time, God planned the victory a little differently. Over the years, God had delivered His people by His hand and that enabled his people to overcome their enemies, but often, Israel took the glory for themselves and laid claim that they delivered themselves with their hardened hearts.

God said to Gideon at the start that he will conquer the Midianites as one man (see Judges 6:16). Can you imagine the look on Gideon's face when the angel of the Lord said that? Gideon must have been pale in his face and thinking to himself, "How will I conquer 135,000 men by myself...?"

You can see the faith Gideon had even to attempt this task. Gideon was to give a peace offering to the angel of the Lord (Jesus). He lit a fire from rocks and showed Gideon that He was a supernatural being. (We know rocks do not burn from tinder and wood!) He cooked Gideon's offering from the fiery rocks—cool, right? But that was not enough encouragement for Gideon.

Gideon then asked the Lord for a sign; he put a fleece, like a type of blanket from an animal, on the ground (see Judges 6:36-38). He prayed and basically said to the Lord, "If the fleece is wet in the morning, but all the ground is dry, then I'll know then that you will save Israel by my hand." The following day, Gideon found that only the fleece was wet, which was very unusual because night dew would usually make everything wet!

Jesus's love and patience encouraged Gideon, but that was still not enough to be a sure sign for him. He then prayed and said to God, "Be not angry, but now this night, let the fleece be dry and make the ground wet," and God did that (see Judges 6:39-40).

We see His kindness toward Gideon. He could have said, "No, you have witnessed me make a fire when I touched your meat with my staff, and you saw me face to face. Then I did as you prayed for a sign to wet the fleece, a sign that goes against natural laws." Jesus was not angered, but rather, He was understanding and loving to reveal these signs to help Gideon believe the words He said.

Fast forward some time when Gideon was to fight the battle, and again the Lord said, "If you are fearful, go down to the camp and listen to a dream one of the soldiers had; his interpretation will give you strength!" (see Judges 7:9-15). Then Gideon dared to march up to an army of 135,000 with just an army of three hundred men. The Lord had refined Gideon's small army for the victory of Israel. They marched not even with a sword in hand, but with trumpets, and they shouted, "The sword of the Lord and Gideon!" (see Judges 7:20).

Could you imagine what would be going through their heads if they were in their carnal understanding when they were to encounter an army that could kill them in about five minutes? They had no weapons, but they had faith in Jesus! The Lord delivered them and turned the entire Midianite army against themselves. They killed one another in confusion and fear of one another. The Lord had sent victory to Gideon and his small, loyal army. God proclaimed the word and Gideon acted. Although at first, there was much hesitancy, great encouragement followed. The Lord saw Gideon's timeline and made him become a valiant leader with integrity for the Lord, and he helped deliver Israel with God's hand.

God played Gideon's life out as a movie reel is spread out, and He called out the mighty man of valour that was in him before Gideon knew it was there! With some training and Gideon's faith in His ability to save Israel, God worked it out for good to deliver His people from slavery, abuse, and famine. Jesus knows how to give someone faith when they need it and to bring out the best in people's characters by faith. God sees differently from a man's viewpoint, and that's why love, patience, and longsuffering are valuable assets as a leader to equip and strengthen us in what we need.

Gideon went to conquer the land that opposed God. Only love could see through the fear and distrust Gideon had at the start to be able to bring out the valiant character Jesus had placed within him.

CHAPTER 18

Without Grace, It's Not Possible

Grace is often overlooked in the world. It can be often misunderstood or even forgotten about. Society can have an "eye for an eye" mentality. Grace is a quality of one of the highest values in life, yet it rarely shows in today's values. A biblical definition of grace is essential: it's unmerited favour, something we do not deserve and cannot work for.

For example, if someone were to rob you of your money on the street, it would be a frightening moment that could leave scars of pain. But imagine police were to find this thief, and they brought him to the police station so you could identify him. The police informed you that this person of interest fits the description. He has prior history; one more mistake, and it's strike three. He will be sentenced to twenty-five years in jail. But imagine you see this young man and decide not to press charges. You see the hurt and pain and the circumstances surrounding his life and the hardship that he has gone through. He does not deserve any forgiveness; he does not deserve your understanding. He deserves to go to jail for his crimes. That is justice, right? Many people in society would agree with you. But what if there is another way that can heal both you and him to work it out for good so a change can take place?

Instead of locking him up to make sure he will not rob anyone for the next twenty-five years guaranteed, what if instead the man can be changed from the inside out? That is where grace can come in with its transformation power. He's been caught, but you choose to ask the police if he will have a sit down with you. You can talk and get to know him as a person, find out why he did the things he has done and what led him to that desperate act.

This is where grace and forgiveness can make a profound difference in people's lives. This is where change can happen, and seeds of love can start. He may be touched by the thought of being spared and want to know who you are and why you care about him.

We really cannot judge another person's footsteps until we have walked in them. And to be honest, we never will; we are all different, and all have experienced different hurts. Instead of throwing away the key, we may need to give time, love, direction, and comfort. Grace is the best approach to making a difference in people's hearts because it reveals love to the broken person's nature that can, in turn, give hope to their souls for change.

If the person goes to jail, twenty-five years of hatred and built-up anger toward society may be released when he gets out. Strict judgment is not always the answer. It may be a cause and effect to drive a worse crime than before because his life would be absolutely ruined by having no hope.

The power of hope is so essential, and with hope can come a change of attitude that leads to repentance. The incorrect punishment can lead to hatred and fuel more anger, if not properly measured out.

Could you imagine if God gave us no option for salvation? Where would the hope be? How would we really behave if He did not give us any grace? We would turn back to the flesh and try to fulfil its desires until judgment comes. What would be the point in wanting to change if we are to meet our doom anyway?

Where there is no empowerment for positive prospects of change, there will eventually be hopelessness. It would be easy to be able to justify one's actions because they have nothing to live for and simply give up and give into all vile actions. I think the core root of many issues in this life and the way some issues are handled are not always correct. For example, if one has cancer, one can look to chemotherapy to solve the issue, but in the process, it can destroy the healthy cells also.

But what if the issue could be corrected before chemotherapy was needed? Let's call chemo "prison," where the system can lock one up in hopes of achieving the end result of a cure. It's not always efficient, it can cause a lot more harm, and the cancer may not even respond.

While going directly to the core of the issue and removing the "cancer" can take a little more manpower and time to begin with and require more skill to remove, in the long run, it can be more beneficial to the offender.

Grace can remove the tainted fallen human nature and its roots that led that person to commit such a crime. That person is in a fallen spiritual state of sin and is blinded. In order to resolve those issues, there needs to be spiritual healing or cleansing of past hurts, and wrong motives in the heart need to be changed.

Grace is the only prospect for making that change. When one gives kindness to their enemy, it can change them and convict them of their sins, so they can be humbled and feel remorse that they have done wrong. Repentance and grace then can shine as hope, and we can know what the power of hope can do.

"If your enemy is hungry, give him bread to eat;
And if he is thirsty, give him water to drink;
For *so* you will heap coals of fire on his head,
And the LORD will reward you."

(Proverbs 25:21-22)

The seed of grace can be sewn into this person's heart for a chance to be loved and cared for. Many people can be caught in this system, and it is a destructive pattern caused by a lack of grace that has enabled this person who was misunderstood to endure further pain for himself and all those he is in contact with. What this person needs is hope and acceptance of who he is so he can then desire to be remorseful and ask for forgiveness.

You may be saying, "So this random person I've never met who tried to rob and assault me, now you want me to help them with love?" Yes, with wisdom of course, but this is what Jesus teaches us!

"'You have heard the law that says, "Love your neighbor" and hate your enemy. But I say, love your enemies! Pray for those who persecute you! In that way, you will be acting as true children of your Father in heaven. For he gives his sunlight to both the evil and the good, and he sends rain on the just and the unjust alike. If you love only those who love you, what reward is there for that? Even corrupt tax collectors do that much. If you are kind only to your friends, how are you different from anyone else? Even pagans do that. But you are to be perfect, even as your Father in heaven is perfect.'"

(Matthew 5:43-48 NLT)

This is where biblical grace can be lacking in society or if we look at the justice systems. It's a risk; it's time, money, and human resources. It's issues that may not yield quick results, but the long-term effects will reduce inmate population. Biblical counselling and grace can change people's cores from the inside; a true repentance caused by grace and knowing Jesus can have a massive impact as we saw with the cartel gang members who were in prison.

Grace is not always the best approach; people can try to manipulate this system. There will always be those who are evil who rightly deserve sentences as well. It's not black and white. But the way some governments run justice systems at the moment can be costly in the long run with ongoing inmate jail housing, feeding, relocating, re-admittance, and with a high number of return offenders. A system that seems to not really rehabilitate anymore but equips people to become harder after their imprisonment by associations is not always the answer.

The modern justice systems already use a massive number of resources that seems to be enlarging every year while crime rates are growing. It's not fixing anything; rather it's housing very hurt and angry people who have been hurt by the devil and are enslaved by him, and there is not much being done to reveal the truth that sets you free (see John 8:32). But there is a better system, and it's called knowing Jesus. Sin, pain, rejection, and being segregated from society can lead to drug use and a lack of purpose in life. It can create a repetitive, hurtful cycle of years of more pain that creates more hurt people. Love is the best way to open the hearts of the lost.

"'The Spirit of the Lord GOD *is* upon Me,
Because the LORD has anointed Me
To preach good tidings to the poor;
He has sent Me to heal the brokenhearted,
To proclaim liberty to the captives,
And the opening of the prison to *those who are* bound;
To proclaim the acceptable year of the LORD,
And the day of vengeance of our God;
To comfort all who mourn,
To console those who mourn in Zion,
To give them beauty for ashes,
The oil of joy for mourning,
The garment of praise for the spirit of heaviness;
That they may be called trees of righteousness,
The planting of the LORD, that He may be glorified.'"

(Isaiah 61:1-3)

Jesus came for the brokenhearted and to give liberty to the captives! We have all been imprisoned by sin, and if we are not found in Jesus, we are then captives under sin. Jesus is our deliverance from the power of darkness and sin that leads to spiritual death and judgment. If the core of a person is transformed, change can take place.

Let's go to a prison in Louisiana, where a warden understood that many who were coming through his gates were lost and hurt, and how he allowed the gospel to change their lives.

Angola prison was once named the bloodiest prison in America. It was known to have been home to some of the most brutal criminals. The state of Louisiana once had a life sentence without parole for a maximum of about ten years until 1972, but in 1979 that sentence for life changed, then there was a momentum shift to twenty years, then forty years without parole. [12] It then became abolished altogether, and life now means you spend the rest of your life behind prison walls if you are convicted. It's sad to see the lack of grace given to people who have been convicted.

Some are definitely just sentences, no doubt. But others can be from a serious mistake made when they were in their youth that keeps them behind bars till natural death. There was a warden there who had the reins of the prison from 1975 to 2016. He is a Christian; he believes a heart can change through knowing Jesus Christ and His transformative power. Before we get to his story, let's have a

---

[12] "Louisiana Lawmakers Pass Bill to Provide Parole Eligibility to Some Elderly 'Lifers,'" Equal Justice Initiative, published June 6, 2021, https://eji.org/news/louisiana-lawmakers-pass-bill-to-provide-parole-eligibility-to-some-elderly-lifers/.

quick rundown on the human condition and how the Bible shares with us that the unrepentant heart is always going to be wicked until Christ reveals grace.

"The heart *is* deceitful above all *things*,
And desperately wicked;
Who can know it?"

(Jeremiah 17:9)

The human mind, body, and soul are darkened from sin. There is sin we do not always control. Some are better than others with how far they allow sin to take them in their actions. All sin is wicked, but it can be expressed in many different ways. It's not just violent crimes that we see most inmates convicted for. We have all been infected by the fallen nature of sin, and the very essence of our core is affected. The only remedy is Christ's power working in us.

His love overcomes evil. He overcame evil by showing love to us when we did not deserve it. His grace drives our empowerment to become better men and women. The Holy Spirit is the powerhouse for our victory over our sinful urges. Jesus has accepted us as we are, and He sees the best in us— just like Gideon—to be able to overcome life's issues.

He knows our inner secrets and fears and has searched for our good or bad inner thoughts. It's genuinely astonishing if we are honest with ourselves that one could love such sinners as us. But Jesus does, and He reveals Himself to people each day in their sins, and He turns their lives around by His grace.

The warden understood this biblical principle that coming to the knowledge of Christ is the only way. Yet, while many inmates were to lose their entire life in a prison cell, the warden offered what he could within his power to deliver a free gospel to all inmates, an eternal life without shame or hurt and with forgiveness and love shown. Eternal life will give hope that not all is lost and that you can be washed as white as snow.

Before 2010, the death penalty was still used in the state of Louisiana. The warden, whose job was to look after the prison and to help prisoners be rehabilitated, had watched a man be put to death because he was on death row for his crime.[13] When this man was given an injection to stop his heart, the warden realised he had forgotten about his spiritual responsibility as a believer. He did his job overseeing the procedure as he watched the process take place, but the man looked fearful of what was about to happen.

The warden thought to himself, "Did I just allow a man to go to hell for eternity without sharing the gospel with him?" Since that day, whenever an inmate was to be put to death, the warden made sure he shared the gospel message with a heartfelt one-on-one talk. He remembers sharing with many prisoners the gospel and sharing the forgiveness of sins and the grace Jesus has to offer.

One hardened criminal, who had fatally shot a woman and paralysed a man whom he was robbing, was to be put to death. For years, the conflict was painful for both parties and involved court hearings and daily reminders of the

---

[13] Dennis Shere, "Warden saw only one answer for troubled La. prison: Christ." January 3, 2008. *Baptist Press*: https://www.baptistpress.com/resource-library/news/warden-saw-only-one-answer-for-troubled-la-prison-christ/ *(May 23, 2022).*

consequences and misfortunes. The victim had lost their partner over a thief's homicide and found himself confined to a life in a wheelchair. At the same time, the offender was sentenced to the death penalty and shame.

The warden spoke with the offender before his execution date and asked him if he wanted to accept Jesus as his saviour and repent of his sins. They both prayed with tears running down their faces, and sinner was made right with Jesus, and there was celebration over his soul joining the kingdom of God. Moments before the man was to be executed, he spoke to the warden and said, "Please tell the man I shot I am sorry for what I did to him and his girlfriend," as sincere tears that rolled down his cheeks. The warden whispered back, "He said he forgives you," as the man was in the viewing area watching the execution.

Jesus' forgiveness has no partiality. He will forgive anyone who will turn to Him in repentance. As like with the two criminals who were crucified with Jesus on either side of Him. It's never too late, and grace will be there as an open hand to catch sinners who seek His mercy.

"Then one of the criminals who were hanged blasphemed Him, saying, 'If You are the Christ, save Yourself and us.'

"But the other, answering, rebuked him, saying, 'Do you not even fear God, seeing you are under the same condemnation? And we indeed justly, for we receive the due reward of our deeds; but this Man has done nothing wrong.' Then he said to Jesus, 'Lord, remember me when You come into Your kingdom.'

"And Jesus said to him, 'Assuredly, I say to you,
today you will be with Me in Paradise.'"

(Luke 23:39-43)

A true repentant heart shows and asks forgiveness. Jesus was on the cross with the two convicted thieves and one was sincere. Humility and the fear of God can lead to repentance and will result in a change in one's behaviour.

Jesus forgave the murderer in the Angola prison, and the man left in the wheelchair was able to come to peace with forgiving and letting that heavy wound start to heal. He had the grace to let the warden know the convicted murderer was forgiven.

True healing took place in that situation, and justice was met. In this world, he paid the price of his sins through our justice system, but he went to be with Jesus as a new man, made right by faith in Jesus, and with the taint of sin taken away by Jesus's mercy to start his life anew as he hoped for in heaven. Often it takes challenging situations in life for us to come to the point that breaks us, so we will want to repent. That is the beauty of grace, but if no grace is shown, it leaves very little room for mindsets to be adjusted.

In the period of time that the warden was involved in running Angola prison, the crime rate within the prison dropped significantly. Offenders who had not received life in prison had a much lower return rate and more had rehabilitated lives. The prison grew with Bible studies each week and larger numbers attended meetings. Drug use and illicit behaviour was greatly diminished. It turned from one of the hardest prisons in America into one with some areas of open living and where responsibilities were given.

Inmates earned GEDs and became part of communities again.

This warden treated the issue of sin rather than punishing the nature of the fallen flesh. It's still a prison, but many inmates were reformed, and new church buildings were built for the new converts. Daily Christian radio broadcasts were set up by the inmates with the gospel message and spiritual music being aired to thousands.

We see today in society how sin has taken hold of communities. If the world continues to accept evil, we will see sharp declining morals, and it will always be a cat and mouse scenario. Societies need to embrace the removal of sin by Christ, and the transformative power that can live within us.

> "Righteousness exalts a nation,
> But sin *is* a reproach to *any* people."
>
> (Proverbs 14:34)

Since grace is a positive enabler of righteous behaviour, it is the unmerited grace that reveals the love of God in our hearts. If that is the way God chose to deal with the human condition (sin), we should look closely at how grace can shape our lives around us.

I love this acronym for the word grace:
God's
Riches
At
Christ's
Expense

Christ is a master of showing us His love. He builds us up to become not what we see, but rather what God sees. We have genuinely inherited the riches of the kingdom by His love and actions on the cross that can deal with the world's problems if we only obey and submit to love.

People can have problems with religion because of the bad stigma created by false ideas and individuals. Many false churches and overzealous people have not acted in love toward Christ's cause, and many millions of people have received an incorrect impression of who Jesus is. It's essential that we can see the true love of who Christ is and what He offered to us on Calvary. He has dealt with sin, the cause and effect of life issues, and now there is an answer: Jesus!

If we are humble and ready to listen to the gospel that represents peace, it can allow the whole context of the Word of God and His character into our lives. His Word will shape and change us. We can see the overall view of His plan for the redemption of man and the heavenly promises to those who ask for mercy. The fallen nature is at enmity with God. People can shoot themselves in the foot by rejecting the love of God and not wanting to open their hearts to understand because of pride. God gave the gospel to all, but usually the brokenhearted and people who are lost are the ones open to the gospel. The less we have here, the more ready we are to lose what we can have in this life for an eternal one. God's kingdom is there if we humble ourselves and are open to His truths as a child is. To trust and obey in love is the only way!

Pride is the enemy of Christ, and unbelief is a blindfold. How can one believe if they are willing to reject truth and allow themselves to be deceived? Humility and grace open the door of the human heart to plant the seeds of the gospel, and the delivery method is often grace to captivate our attention!

CHAPTER 19

A Change in Perspective

Many people see religion as boring and lifeless. It's even seen as a burden at times by those who do not understand Christ's love. While it is true there are serious aspects to salvation with wars against sin and darkness, ultimately, it is to bring people into the kingdom of God. I believe heaven will be full of joy, peace, and laughing and getting to enjoy family like when we were kids and then we often reminisce about our favourite childhood memories with our loved ones. When hardship is in the world, it can be difficult to remember the positive things that happened long before life's issues. There are many positive aspects in life if we can change our view of the negative.

Life's essence is harmony. For example, when we explore God's nature, we can see His personality from what He has created. When we are in sorrow and pain, we tend to have horse blinkers on, and we can only see the opposing views that are against God, like why bad things happen and all those questions that can try to rush through our minds to be at enmity and cause conflict within our hearts and to try to impose moral standards on God (see Isaiah 45:9, Romans 9:20).

There is usually much more good than bad in life. We can take for granted good family times, holidays, success, fulfilment in work, and all day-to-day aspects. We as humans can be subject to our surroundings. For example, a person in war can be longing for the sounds of tranquillity and silence and to have no war planes overhead or bombs exploding. We all have luxuries in this life that can easily be overlooked compared to nations at war. We can sometimes allow negative aspects to try to dominate our minds and try to get us to question God's grace.

A thirsty man in a desert can be seeking just one drop of water on his dry tongue to soothe the desire for refreshment. Yet we can abundantly waste our comforts and often overlook the small blessings in life, but someone's small blessings are someone's bigger blessings when longing and desires meet the essence of life and the sustaining grace from God.

It's a part of life that we have daily access to God's grace. It rains on the just and the unjust (see Matthew 5:45). When things do not go our way, we can often be blindsided by negativity that fills our minds and allows the bad to outweigh the good. The higher the standard of living with abundant conditions the more we become desensitised by our comforts, and we usually only see the negatives in a bigger light because of the lack of resilience toward hardships that may present themselves. People who have been in hardships for years can become tender toward God's mercies and the beautiful scenery that He has given us, to be more aware of the smaller blessings in life, and then we can see the finer acts of God's grace within all of our lives. We will soon cover Paul's approach with a stoic like mind with life's issues and being able to see the positive that God's mercies offer us for eternal joy that gives us strength in all life's hard situations, so we can have a brighter perspective through the riches of Christ and our inheritance. Stoicism was not his religious belief, but more a mere approach of strength toward the faith of Jesus and the best way to fight the good fight of faith and to allow his walk to approach the tactics of the wicked one, the rewards that Jesus richly taught to have an eternal perceptive, and to see that God works all things for good.

> "For the weapons of our warfare *are* not carnal but mighty in God for pulling down strongholds, casting down arguments and every high thing that exalts itself against the knowledge of God, bringing every thought into captivity to the obedience of Christ."
>
> (2 Corinthians 10:4-5)

There is a battlefield, and the battlefield is in our minds. Our minds are the ground for thoughts, reasons, beliefs, and actions. Our minds are powerful, and what we allow to dictate to us can shape us for the positive or the negative. We see the Bible shares in Corinthians that we are at war against demonic powers that try to sway and influence people's minds to be darkened toward God. We see the Bible teaches us how the demonic tries to exalt itself and tries to stop us knowing God's truths, by saying, "If God was real..." or "If God did this..." All things the devil used in the garden of Eden:

"[The serpent] said to the woman, 'Has God indeed said, "You shall not eat of every tree of the garden"?'

"And the woman said to the serpent, 'We may eat the fruit of the trees of the garden; but of the fruit of the tree which *is* in the midst of the garden, God has said, "You shall not eat it, nor shall you touch it, lest you die.'"

> "Then the serpent said to the woman,
> 'You will not surely die. For God knows that
> in the day you eat of it your eyes will be opened,
> and you will be like God, knowing good and evil.'"
>
> (Genesis 3:1-5)

It's important that we take all these thoughts captive that try to steal our joy and peace. Knowledge is powerful, and the knowledge of Jesus results in salvation. The devil can try to stop Christians or non-believers from experiencing God's fullness due to questioning God and rebelling. This is where trusting God allows Him to work all things for good in our lives.

If we question God and start to allow our perspectives and hurts to dictate who and what God should be doing, we are creating an idol of who we think God should be for us, rather than experiencing the true God and submitting to His order and trusting Him to bring life and love from the midst of a decaying world. Promise, faith, and endurance are the reality of our Christian faith for the better kingdom to be ushered in.

If we allow Jesus to change our view of how we see the world, we can have greater hope in this life. If we compare ourselves with people who have rejected Christ and have chosen to go to hell, they have no hope for ever. It will be a never-ending doom and separation from God. How hopeful are our lives and perspectives of His grace if we take a thoughtful moment to look at the light of hope we have and the remission of sins to really promote the joy of a greater life to come!

A little while back, I was watching some YouTube videos. I stumbled across a video that touched my heart. The description was titled "colour blind people see colour for the first time!!" I thought to myself, "I'll watch their reactions. Why not?" For my amusement, I thought it would be great to see people's reactions for the first time and to see colours they never once could. To my amazement, when people put on the glasses that allowed them to see the correct colours, many started to cry with joy and had emotional responses. To me who had always taken the colours of life for granted, I never thought much of it. But all they saw was pure beauty, beautiful, vivid and distinct colours. Life was now vibrant in a world of possibilities they hadn't seen before. It was a paradigm change, and boy, it brought joy!

As tears were coming down their faces, tears of happiness started to roll down my cheeks! I kept clicking on the new YouTube suggestions with more and more colour-blind people and their reactions. I never understood how some people saw many colours as the same colour! All they saw was different shades of bland shades, and sometimes they could not distinguish flowers in the grass or minor aspects or details that we often take for granted. That revealed the blessing of life to me.

We can take for granted the beauty in life we all get to enjoy. We have a free gift of life and to be able to see God's wonders. Life can be short, and often our perspective can be narrow-minded like horse blinkers. It's so easy for us to take the blessings we have for granted.

To see this world from a different perspective took some hard life lessons for me. From my personal experience, when I left my hospital room after the ordeal I endured with the pulmonary embolism, I snuck outside to get a short breath of fresh summer air and to experience life's precious qualities. It was a much-needed gasp to take in a breath of air with contentment that I was still alive, and to hear the birds' singing echoing in my ears was the sweetness of peace. It was a vivid experience of life and God's qualities of mercy that I was alive to see His goodness; even though I was still partly blinded by darkness and my life was yet to be revealed in Christ, God was working on my hardened heart.

I saw the vivid colours in a short glimpse of life's precious qualities that have stayed with me ever since, a glow of His love and creativity. We realize we have an amazing creator when we can see God's right perspective in this life. Even through trials in life, there can still be beautiful opportunities to see God's grace, as I had experienced after just making it down the short hallway and elevator by myself to get the summer sun on my face. But that experience of God's grace was not enough for me until life's bumpy journeys eventually led me to the path of being born again and accepting Jesus Christ as saviour and I was baptised with His Holy Spirit.

I had now been given the Holy Spirit's glasses (so to speak), the eternal gift of knowing what He has truly done for me and that He is love! What power perspectives can hold. Perspectives can change our outlook on life and what truly really matters. As I said before, many people see religion as boring. I understand because I was once in that mindset, but that is from a perspective with the wrong shades on—let's say darkened shades for now.

I don't like the word religion. It's so misunderstood with man's attempts to do things their way and not God's ways. In plain terms, it means to believe in a higher power, and that's true. I do, but I want to be associated with being like Jesus, not being religious. If we look at words and the different meanings they can hold, it's interesting that the same word, over different generations and cultures, can morph into different meanings for different age brackets.

"Nice" used to mean "silly or foolish." [14] "Awful" used to mean "worthy of awe," [15] and "silly" used to indicate "blessed." How things have changed!

I often say, I'm a Christian who has a relationship with Jesus, I'm not religious as some may try to brand me as, but it's a lifestyle of knowing who Love is! I think it's time for the world's idea of the word religion to change from being a believer in a higher power, to being associated with traditions and rule of man, not Christianity. Many people have been hurt by religion, but that's not God's will. It has been man's decisions to act on behalf of God without proper context or relationship with God.

But, as we live with spiritual perspectives, people with the dark shades often see church activity as silly, tedious, and controlled by strict leaders who try to take the fun out of any activities. Jesus was the opposite of religious, if I dare

---

[14] Clare Toeniskoetter, "The changing meanings of 'nice' and 'silly,'" Michigan Radio, published Oct. 27, 2013, https://www.michiganradio.org/arts-culture/2013-10-27/the-changing-meanings-of-nice-and-silly

[15] "Awful," Online Etymology Dictionary, https://www.etymonline.com/word/awful, Aug. 4, 2022.

put it that way for the modern understanding of that word. Did you know He would condemn and question religious leaders and fight for what is right, going against the religious leaders of those days who opposed God and chose to obey man and rules rather than the God who gives life. The religious leaders were the ones who killed Jesus on the cross, after all, because they thought themselves to be holy and righteous in their own efforts. But luckily that was allowed and ordained to happen so we can receive remission of sins! (See 1 Corinthians 2:8.)

Perspectives change lives and the true meaning of life is meant to be seen with vivid colours that pop to life from God's perspective. We are to see all the beauty in Jesus, but the life of the sinful, fallen nature corrupts us in ways that can lead us away in duplicity. We can be tricked by what is not necessarily important, and we trade the riches for decaying rot. But if we change our glasses, we can see the true values in life. Once, it would probably have taken someone giving me $100 in order to get me to read maybe half a chapter of the Bible.

Now I'm learning the false perspectives of this life, and there are often tempting lures to try and get us away from true riches. Now when I go into the Bible, it's as if I am reading a treasure map of wisdom that will guide me into knowing Jesus more intimately and to seek His love. It is all eternal lessons from an eternal God who has given instructions to me, but not only me, but all who choose to seek out His knowledge that changes people's lives for the good.

Yet many Christians also lack knowledge of the Word of God. Not all, but there are many who fail to read their

Bibles as disciples. Have many been dulled to the point of boredom? I think not. Rather, have some hearts grown lukewarm and more interested in the lust of the eyes and pride of life than caring for the knowledge of the Holy One of Israel?

"Do not love the world or the things in the world. If anyone loves the world, the love of the Father is not in him. For all that *is* in the world—the lust of the flesh, the lust of the eyes, and the pride of life—is not of the Father but is of the world. And the world is passing away, and the lust of it; but he who does the will of God abides forever."

(1 John 2:15-17)

Perspectives are worth changing, and with change can come a newfound love. The master, Jesus Christ, and His simplicity of faith and grace can fill our hearts with His selfless love and mercy. We can experience His creation from a correct view that enlightens this world and can empower forceful changes within culture to explore the greater realities of God!

I think of people who dream about space travel and exploring the outer edges of our galaxies with telescopes, scientists who search intently for the key to it all with the microcosms of the fabric of reality, or archaeologists who look back in time for clues and knowledge. Correct perspectives can fill in hidden mysteries that the world was once darkened to. Like eyes in a dark room slowly adjusting to the light, new ideas can be explored with God taking the shades off and revealing His truths. What progress could be made with understanding who God is and seeing His awe and wonder within all designs of life.

> "Declaring the end from the beginning,
> And from ancient times *things* that are not *yet* done."
>
> (Isaiah 46:10)

The creator of heaven and Earth shares His knowledge, and His living word is verified with ancient texts that bring forth spiritual well-being and peace that reveals the key to eternal life, Jesus! It has knowledge of things to come and things that have passed, stamped with the authenticity of the One who declared the end events to show the reality of our faith. Understanding the world and how God framed it unlocks mysteries to generations! There is a piece that will interest every single person on the face of the Earth if we seek God and His ways.

> "'Let your heart retain my words;
> Keep my commands, and live.
> Get wisdom! Get understanding!
> Do not forget, nor turn away from the words of my mouth.
> Do not forsake her, and she will preserve you;
> Love her, and she will keep you.
> Wisdom *is* the principal thing;
> *Therefore* get wisdom.
> And in all your getting, get understanding.
> Exalt her, and she will promote you;
> She will bring you honor, when you embrace her.
> She will place on your head an ornament of grace;
> A crown of glory she will deliver to you.'"
>
> (Proverbs 4:4-9)

Those are captivating words from God. It's His living word, and it is so influential. Within the texts, it can become conceptualised in our minds and formulated into life by the power of His Spirit. Belief and trust in the living God give us His knowledge, which humans have sought for thousands of years. God gives us answers on what we need to know and what is beneficial for His will to be done on Earth. His Word trains and equips us in the ways of the Lord, giving life lessons we can relate to and grow with so we can benefit from others who have experienced their faith being tested, like many of the authors in the Bible. Wisdom and understanding are on each page, which is designed to empower us and help us in our walk with Jesus and to know His love.

The Bible is our guidebook and our treasure map in this life. The hope we can have is through Jesus. Without Christ, there is no hope, no joy, no love, and nothing to look forward to after death. Just a matter of a vain existence in a vast universe full of meaningless life with no answers and impending judgment. It's not who Jesus is nor is it what He wants for us. Life is meant to be vibrant, and the gospel is a matter of sharing and giving people a view from our glasses of faith that allow understanding and wisdom to come into one's life to reveal the fullness of joy.

There's a reason why some reborn Christian inmates on death row can sing songs to Jesus before they are executed. It's because they have their spiritual glasses on to see the kingdom of God. They are a new creation, and all sins are forgiven and forgotten, they are ready to be with their master Jesus. We can see Christians in court rooms forgiving their child's murderer and giving them a hug with tears, or charities receiving goods and grace; it's a reflection of Jesus Christ within Christians to shine who God is and His forgiveness.

We can see in the Scriptures the first martyr, Stephen, was killed for sharing His faith. His story comes to mind with being able to see the kingdom of heaven and Jesus at the right hand of God. Stephen was stoned to death. Rocks were hitting his body and slowly rupturing his blood vessels, breaking his ribs, tearing chunks of flesh from his body, and delivering blunt force trauma to his head, but we see what the Bible reveals Stephen did in his last breaths on Earth.

"But he, being full of the Holy Spirit, gazed into heaven and saw the glory of God, and Jesus standing at the right hand of God, and said, 'Look! I see the heavens opened and the Son of Man standing at the right hand of God!'

"Then they cried out with a loud voice, stopped their ears, and ran at him with one accord; and they cast *him* out of the city and stoned *him*. And the witnesses laid down their clothes at the feet of a young man named Saul. And they stoned Stephen as he was calling on *God* and saying, 'Lord Jesus, receive my spirit.' Then he knelt down and cried out with a loud voice, 'Lord, do not charge them with this sin.' And when he had said this, he fell asleep."

(Acts 7:55-60)

What amazing love and the grace Stephen had while he was being stoned to death. He had the spiritual glasses Jesus gave him. He could see eternal life and the grace that implored him to yell out, "Do not charge them with this sin!" Stephen knew the devil's shades blinded the religious leaders. The truth Stephen spoke about who God was hurt the religious leaders, yet they denied the truth and replaced it with a lie (see Romans 1:25). Only God can give people the kind of love to cry out for forgiveness for their killers while being murdered. It's only a love that can be credited to Jesus.

The religious leaders' pride had stopped them from knowing the actual value of life. They thought their wisdom and knowledge were superior to others and therefore made them better than others. In today's society, some religions reject the holiness of God and His will and can exchange Him for their own god, made from their own imagination that suits their own desires. In Jesus's time, they were called sons of the devil (see John 8:44).

Paul, the soon-to-be apostle, was later recruited into the family of God. He was the overseer and instigator of Stephen's death. He had authority to kill new Christian believers. It was authority ordained by the religious leaders, not God. We see in Scripture that when Jesus appeared to Paul on the Damascus road, He rebuked him and said to him, "It *is* hard for you to kick against the goads" (Acts 9:5).

That was a term for a sharp object that the farmers would often use against cattle if they wanted to be stubborn and stop pulling the harvesting equipment. Jesus was telling him it is vanity and a waste of time to be killing His Christians. In that visitation, Paul was blinded by the glory of the Lord. Later on, we know that Paul received his sight after a person called Ananias prayed for him to receive his sight back.

"'Brother Saul, the Lord Jesus, who appeared to you on the road as you came, has sent me that you may receive your sight and be filled with the Holy Spirit.' Immediately there fell from his eyes *something* like scales, and he received his sight at once; and he arose and was baptised."

(Acts 9:17-18)

Something like scales fell from Paul's eyes and he was opened to the truth. He was baptised in the Spirit and was filled with the Holy Spirit. He was a leader who was once extreme to the point of murdering his fellow countrymen, but he was changed by Jesus! Paul became enlightened by the power of Jesus on the Damascus road. God removed from him the spiritual blindness of the devil and opened his mind and heart to see the true and living God. Who better but apostle Paul to teach the verses below than one who was blinded, but now he sees, just like the song, "Amazing Grace"!

"But even if our gospel is veiled, it is veiled to those who are perishing, whose minds the god of this age has blinded, who do not believe, lest the light of the gospel of the glory of Christ, who is the image of God, should shine on them."

(2 Corinthians 4:3-4)

When Jesus opens the spiritually blind eyes, they can see the colours of new hope. To have hope is a new experience that they had never realised how much they were in need of. What a joy to see the full spectrum of colours, and that is the joy and celebration Christians can share in fellowship. To have all things in common: Christ! He merges all types regardless of who we have been or who we are. He pours His love into our hearts (see Romans 5:5).

Just when I was praying to Jesus, as I covered briefly before, and my heart cried out to him in prayer, I said, "Lord, say anything to me; I just want to hear your voice—even just say my name." His love is true, and He met me with my cry. He said my name with colours of love in His timing. That is how Jesus sees all of us if we will let Him. He has a way of giving us the love we need and shows us that interpersonal relationship we desire and thirst after. When the creation meets their maker, God's love is poured out for our hearts to be renewed in love.

CHAPTER 20
The Faithful One

Without faithfulness, there can be no hope. As humans, we can often be unfaithful in the small and big things; it's something God wants us to address by His power. It's a part of our old nature with the fallen condition. But love is faithful, and with faithfulness comes a place to trust.

A fortified place where we can look for help is what Jesus will give us, and He cares to give us rest for our souls. A renewal of love is what's needed in the human heart. As we have covered before, the love of God is poured out into our hearts. But by experiencing His love, we can come to rest on His faithful characteristics.

We can see a different type of faithfulness. It's not man's—rather, it's God's. We know the Bible constantly reveals to us His faithfulness. Let's have a look at Abraham's story and how God was faithful. I love this event that is told to us in the Bible. We can see a part of Jesus's character like not many other examples in the Bible.

"Then God said to Abraham, 'As for Sarai your wife, you shall not call her name Sarai, but Sarah shall be her name. And I will bless her and also give you a son by her; then I will bless her, and she shall be *a mother of* nations; kings of peoples shall be from her.'

"Then Abraham fell on his face and laughed, and said in his heart, "Shall *a child* be born to a man who is one hundred years old? And shall Sarah, who is ninety years old, bear *a child*?' And Abraham said to God, 'Oh, that Ishmael might live before You!'

"Then God said: "No, Sarah your wife shall bear
you a son, and you shall call his name Isaac.'"
(Genesis 17:15-19)

We see that although Abraham had great reverence for God, as seen when he fell on his face before God when the Lord was blessing him and establishing the covenant with him. But when God said that he and Sarah were to have a son, he fell again on his face with laughter and thought, "Surely not, Lord, we are both nearly one hundred years old."

"'Abraham believed God, and it was accounted to him for righteousness.' And he was called the friend of God."
(James 2:23)

Abraham thought that Ishmael was the son of the promise, who was thirteen at that time. But no, God, with His loving and kind words said, "No, Sarah, your wife, will have a child." It must have been a shock. Although Abraham had been waiting for years for the promise to be fulfilled, he partly thought it was through Ishmael, who was now becoming a man. We see Abraham's relationship with God in this conversation, although he was very respectful and upright toward the Lord with the previous talk about the established covenant. The Lord was now revealing to Abraham the surprise for Sarah and him. The baby was to come from a free woman—representing Jerusalem, who has been set free—not from the bondwoman who was a servant, Hagar, who gave birth to Ishmael. Although both brothers were to become very blessed, it was ordained for Sarah's line to be blessed for the coming Messiah to take the sins from the world.

Abraham was called the friend of God. How more personal can we get to God than becoming His friend? We see a few times that the angel of the Lord (the "sent one") came in His pre-incarnate body and visited Abraham. When the Lord visited Abraham and Sarah, shortly after the first visit with Abraham, Abraham must have rushed back and told Sarah they were to have a child after all these years. The original promise was clarified, no thanks to leaning on their own understanding and bringing Hagar into it. Rather, it will come from the two of them!

Abraham saw the Lord pass by just shortly after the other visitation when Abraham met with the Lord when He was on his way to another town. Abraham quickly said to the Lord, "Please stop by for a meal," so he prepared a meal for Jesus. It's funny: one day, I was chatting with my wife, Whitney, and she said, "Could you imagine cooking a meal for God?"

I never thought about that aspect, but it's true! What would you make? There was no master chef or Google back then to guide you! Abraham served the most delicate lamb with the best bread, sweets, butter, and milk. I'm sure Jesus enjoyed it!

Abraham had the pleasure of hosting such a guest in his humble abode. Abraham and Sarah possibly had a few visitations over the time and could talk with Jesus face to face and create a bond and get to know Jesus's character. When Abraham was ninety-nine years old, about twenty-four years after the promise was given to them that Abraham and Sarah were to have a son, He then declared it again.

"Then they said to him, 'Where *is* Sarah your wife?'

"So he said, 'Here, in the tent.'

"And He said, 'I will certainly return to you according to the time of life, and behold, Sarah your wife shall have a son.'

"(Sarah was listening in the tent door which *was* behind him.) Now Abraham and Sarah were old, well advanced in age; *and* Sarah had passed the age of childbearing. Therefore Sarah laughed within herself, saying, 'After I have grown old, shall I have pleasure, my lord being old also?'

"And the LORD said to Abraham, 'Why did Sarah laugh, saying, "Shall I surely bear *a child*, since I am old?" Is anything too hard for the LORD? At the appointed time I will return to you, according to the time of life, and Sarah shall have a son.'

"But Sarah denied *it*, saying, 'I did not laugh,' for she was afraid."

"And He said, 'No, but you did laugh!'"
(Genesis 17:9-15)

We see Jesus's personality coming out here again, as we see Sarah could laugh, but still keep a reverent fear of God. Sarah unwittingly lied to the Creator to cover her laugh, but she couldn't trick Him! I guess we would all laugh too if we were also nearly one hundred years old when we got that news!

This is a type of relationship Jesus wants to have with His creation, not that we should lie or be unbelieving but to know Him as a friend and to make Him our best friend, to laugh with and cry with Jesus, who is always there for us. His ability, being God, is that He knows all. He is everywhere. He is omniscient (all-knowing), omnipotent (all-powerful), and omnibenevolent (supremely good). When we are looking for a friend, Jesus is always watching us and is with us—living within us and understanding every situation. We can be conscious of His presence that never leaves us—an intimate God who created us for fellowship.

Jesus cares so much about Abraham and Sarah. He loves them with unfailing love and wants to be faithful and to help in all situations. We see God's faithfulness over Abraham's journey and how God was looking after him and Sarah. We ultimately know that Isaac was born, and after twenty-five years, God fulfilled His promise to Abraham and Sarah.

God often rebuked kings for Abraham's sake and led him on a path that not many would have been able to travel. We see over the course of the entire history of Israel that God has kept His word to His people. God promised Abraham to have as many children as the stars that he could count in the sky. God also promised him to have a great nation. And there was a fulfilment of that after the faithfulness of God, who led Moses and the people of Abraham out of Egypt and into the promised land just as God said He would do after four hundred years in captivity. We see Israel became a mighty nation from a small clan called the Israelites. Kings were made from the womb of Sarah, and the King of Kings, Jesus, also came from the seed of Abraham from the promise given to King David to be of his seed.

Let's jump forward a few thousand years after some of the prophets. When Israel was scattered after AD 70 and then again in AD 130, the Romans destroyed Jerusalem, and all people from their land were pushed to the outer edges of the world. For thousands of years, we see that Jerusalem was no longer the people of Israel, and the Jewish communities had minimal regard with the world to become a nation again.

History, over time, has shown us that once a nation has been scattered and broken apart, not many nations have ever come back to power and to rebuild the way Israel has. The city of Jerusalem has been "destroyed twice, attacked 52 times, besieged 23 times, and captured and recaptured 44 times."[16]

It's truly God's hand that has achieved a constant rebuilding and given chances to the Israelites. If they had not rebelled, I'm without a doubt they would have never been defeated, but with rebellion can come judgment. We see some of the old civilizations with the most powerful empires in the world with the most significant numbers have failed to rebuild with similar position in the world as

---

[16] "Timeline of Jerusalem," Wikipedia, last updated Aug. 1, 2022, https://en.wikipedia.org/wiki/Timeline_of_Jerusalem, Aug. 5, 2022

before their destruction. On May 14, 1948, for the first time in history, a nation was born again. In one day, it was revived.

"'Who has heard such a thing?
Who has seen such things?
Shall the earth be made to give birth in one day?
Or shall a nation be born at once?'"

(Isaiah 66:8)

Hundreds of thousands of Hebrews packed out flights and flocked home. There were cargo planes full of people returning home. They left their old lives behind and rebuilt their new homes in Jerusalem. The nation's dialect was restored. This has never happened in history for people to return to their native tongue after being scattered abroad. This is the hand of God. His counsel stands, and His faithfulness is with His people.

God has always had His faithfulness toward Israel in all the Bible prophecy and world events. If we look at major world events, somehow, the Jewish people are often involved. Not by their own doing, but partly because of the destructive nature of man and the hatred toward God and His people. It has been ordained that the nation of Israel will be a great nation. A promise was given by God the Father. It would be naive for us as Christians to leave the Jewish culture and God's faithfulness toward them out of the picture. There is much more to come for conflict with the world and the Abrahamic line; the Bible only reveals more to come, but we know the end story of Jesus being faithful and fighting for the Israelites when the entire world is ready to go to war against them in Revelation.

Another example of God's faithfulness is Joseph, Abraham's great-grandson. When Joseph was a young man, we see he was sold into slavery by his jealous brothers (see Genesis 37). God had shown Joseph that his family would bow down to him as a leader.

Scripture shows us that we should be wise with whom we share things as it can create issues, but in this case, God worked it all out for good. After Joseph was sold into slavery, he became trained in the things of Egypt and became a talented young man. The Lord was with him to guide him to help build Abraham's family tree. Even though his brothers betrayed Joseph and there was much heartache regarding those issues, God had a plan to build Joseph up and exalt him.

Joseph, when experiencing trials, could have said to God, "You promised me that I would become a leader, and my brothers would bow down to me." Not that that is what he was about; he was humble and kind. He could have had questions about why things were the way they were; he was enslaved because of what his brothers did to him.

As time went by, Joseph became prominent and was the leader of his master's house and goods—until he was falsely accused of raping his master's wife (see Genesis 39). We see that Joseph was tempted, but he passed the trial test when she wanted to lay down with him. He said, "No, I will not sin against God." She reacted in hate and anger toward Joseph for refusing to sleep with her. She may have been scared that Joseph, a faithful servant, may have revealed it to the master, so she framed him. Even though Joseph's honesty and integrity led to him being falsely accused, he was much safer in serving his God rather than pleasing himself and being unfaithful toward God and his master's house. It shows us that he was in safety even though he stood up for what he believed and suffered for it; it would have been worse without God's protection.

Now Joseph found himself in prison for seven years. He might have been thinking, "What is all of this? Why am I here? First, I received a blessing from God in visions and dreams, then my brothers tried to kill me and then decided to sell me! Then I was making progress in life and learning the ways of the Egyptian people. Now I'm back worse than before when I was a slave."

In all of this, God was training Joseph to be wise, patient, and humble. He had the dialect of the Egyptians that he learned from in his master's house so he could trade, and then God used him to be the prison guard's right-hand man (see Genesis 39:21-23). In all of this we see God being faithful and training him as a process. Nonetheless, God knew what He was doing for His people to prosper in this new land and how to train Joseph to be a leader.

After a few years in prison, it was time for God to make his name known to the Pharaoh of Egypt. God had given two dreams to some other people in jail with Joseph, and he interpreted the dreams (see Genesis 40). They came to pass and were confirmed. Eventually, word got out to the Pharaoh when he had a few dreams that no one could interpret. Joseph interpreted them correctly, and God's faithfulness was brought forth in Joseph's life. Pharaoh was so glad to understand the interpretation and saw the meaning was true and was from Joseph's God. Pharaoh made him ruler of the entire nation. No one else other than the Pharaoh could overrule him.

We see that God works in ways that may not make sense to us. Often in life, we can question God and be frustrated, but we don't see all the ways God is working in us.

"Then his brothers also went and fell down before his face, and they said, 'Behold, we *are* your servants.'

"Joseph said to them, "Do not be afraid, for *am* I in the place of God? **But as for you, you meant evil against me;** *but* **God meant it for good,** in order to bring it about as *it is* this day, to save many people alive. Now therefore, do not be afraid; I will provide for you and your little ones.' And he comforted them and spoke kindly to them."
(Genesis 50:18-21, emphasis added)

God fulfilled His promise to Joseph and was working all out for good. We see that He was also fulfilling His promise to Abraham in just four generations. God was shaping a nation, a nation that had favour in Egypt through the rule of Joseph. They became mighty and were prospering in what they did. God saved them from the famine in the world and used the evil Joseph's brothers did for good.

> "And we know that all things work together for
> good to those who love God, to those
> who are the called according to *His* purpose."
> (Romans 8:28)

God is faithful; over thousands of years, He has shown His integrity and kept His word to thousands of generations, still up to 1948 with Israel becoming a nation again, which was prophesied nearly three thousand years ago. If we go over the Bible, each account shows us His faithfulness and long-suffering toward us. His faithfulness has a purpose in each book, and it's a journey of knowing His love on each page of the Bible.

"For your kingdom is an everlasting kingdom.
You rule throughout all generations.
The LORD always keeps his promises;
he is gracious in all he does."
(Psalm 145:13 NLT, emphasis added)

"Jesus Christ *is* the same yesterday,
today, and forever."
(Hebrews 13:8)

"'God *is* not a man, that He should lie,
Nor a son of man, that He should repent.
Has He said, and will He not do?
Or has He spoken, and will He not make it good?'"
(Numbers 23:19)

God is outside of time. He does not change: we humans change, but He stays the same. He's a supreme being who does not change His mind and who has wisdom, grace, love, and mercy. This is what the Bible teaches us: His words intertwine and weave through, perfectly meshed and synced. He does not contradict Himself, nor does He lie.

Many authors wrote the Bible, and the base story has always lined up with context. The author is the Holy Spirit, who inspires men to speak and write the words of God.

Let's look at this metaphor of how God sees time. I find it interesting. Charles Spurgeon once stated in one of his sermons that God sees our time as a flowing river.[17] As the river flows, that represents time and God watches from above. He can see the timeline in advance because of His view.

God sees what is coming and He can direct the paths and the flow of water around objects (time moving forward). Since He is outside of time, He has destined and planned all things for good in all our lives when we accept Him, and as we believe in Him, we will belong to Him by our own free choice and allow Him to work in our lives for good according to His plans and purposes.

Spurgeon explained it this way: if one is on a high hill and can see ahead a large ship that is following down a river into the sea, one can see the path the river will take and the curves of the river that the water follows. That is how God can see our timeline of the world and what events will take place ahead as one sees from a bird's eye view, but instead of a river it's our timeline that is linear to God.

To make my own metaphor branched from Spurgeon's idea, just as a fine craftsman can build our lives for our best and for Christ's will to be done here, we need to stay in the boat that is taking us down the river that we call

---

[17] Charles Spurgeon, "God's Estimate of Time - Charles Spurgeon Sermon," YouTube video, 9:40-11:00,
https://www.youtube.com/watch?v=3ut-UVYaFms

life. To be abiding in faith will keep us in God's ship that keeps us safe from the wild storms and seas.

Ships are built with the substructure, then comes the reinforcement, then the ship starts to take shape. The Word of God is the ship that keeps us safe. His Word is also manifold by maintaining the correct co-ordinates for our faith (rudder), and the faith we have is the ship's boards that seal the ship to be called seaworthy. First Timothy 1:19 refers to our faith as a boat to keep on track and to stay off the rocky coast edges. Often, ships need repairs, and we need to have maintenance done to our vessels so we can continue our journey on the river of faith that leads to eternal life. The Word of God maintains our faith. It helps build our most holy faith, so we can continue resting in the boat for our travels.

We see when Jesus was in the boat with His disciples as He was crossing the Sea of Galilee. He was sleeping even though the twelve disciples were afraid. God wants us to be at rest in this journey by knowing the truths He has for us, to be a firm and solid, well-built ship.

When we find rest in storms, we can experience going from faith to faith. The journeys can seem challenging and rigorous, but God plans it all for good, just like Joseph. The Bible talks about faith coming from hearing the Word of God (see Romans 10:17). We can build our trust by seeing the faithfulness of Jesus Christ and how He has demonstrated over history how faithful He is. He doesn't change. We can, and often that can lead the ship's path into storms that can toss it about. But God wants us to keep being faithful, and as we hold on, He will never let us go.

"For if we died with *Him*,
We shall also live with *Him*.
If we endure,
We shall also reign with *Him*.
If we deny *Him*,
He also will deny us.
If we are faithless,
He remains faithful;
He cannot deny Himself."

(2 Timothy 2:12-13)

Even if we are faithless, Scripture tells us He will remain faithful. But we may have a more strenuous ride on the river of life outside of the ship while He destined us to be sitting safely with Jesus in the boat, like how Jesus calmed the storms in the disciples' lives. God wants us to be faithful to Him, and in the end, as we have seen over the Bible's history, blessing follows obedience (see Deuteronomy 28:1-2).

"But you, beloved, building yourselves up on your most holy faith, praying in the Holy Spirit, keep yourselves in the love of God, looking for the mercy of our Lord Jesus Christ unto eternal life."

(Jude 1:20-21)

We are to be praying in the Holy Spirit and keeping ourselves in the love of God by seeking God's mercy and the salvation of our souls. We covered how Jesus is the captain of our souls. We are on the ship in this journey we call life;

we are sojourners searching for our homeland. Jesus is the faithful one who oversees our journey and directs our paths.

"The steps of a *good* man are ordered by the LORD,
And He delights in his way."

(Psalm 37:23)

CHAPTER 21

Christic the Healer

"There are also many other things that Jesus did,
which if they were written one by one, I suppose
that even the world itself could not contain the books
that would be written. Amen."

(John 21:25)

In just three years of Jesus's ministry, He made an impact no one else has had on Earth. We see many examples of Jesus healing the sick in the gospels. Some of the most recorded healings were in the Gospel of Luke. Funnily enough, Luke was a doctor by trade, so it makes sense for Luke to take notice of the more refined detail than the other disciples who documented Christ's miracles. We know Jesus had compassion on large numbers of people. He often wept for them and shared in the laughter with their newfound joy. This is what the gospel is about—showing love and walking in the divine power of the Holy Spirit, sharing the good news with signs following those who believe.

"'Go into all the world and preach the gospel to every
creature. He who believes and is baptised will be saved;
but he who does not believe will be condemned.
And these signs will follow those who believe:
In My name they will cast out demons; they will speak
with new tongues; they will take up serpents; and if they
drink anything deadly, it will by no means hurt them;
they will lay hands on the sick, and they will recover.'"

(Mark 16:15-18)

This is called the Great Commission to all disciples: to
preach the gospel and baptise them to know Christ and
share the living faith by being empowered with fruits and
giftings of the Holy Spirit. Just as Jesus taught His disciples,
He also said all those who believe should make more
disciples. We have the inner working of the Holy Spirit's
power to lay on hands to expect people to recover from
illness just as Jesus healed people.

Christians are supernatural beings, not in a
"superhero" way, but by our faith. We have a supernatural
God who empowers us to share the victory of the cross and
all of its benefits (see Psalm 103:2-5).

"Now faith is the substance of things hoped for, the
evidence of things not seen. For by it the elders obtained a
good testimony.

"By faith we understand that the worlds were framed
by the word of God, so that the things which are
seen were not made of things which are visible."

(Hebrews 11:1-3)

By our faith, we believe. What may not be a reality is made real by our beliefs and faith. Just as Jesus said to family and friends of a dead girl, "Only believe, and she will be made well." People standing by grieving the young girl's death in the Scriptures below saw the reality that this girl was clearly dead. But Jesus said, "No, she is sleeping." Jesus understood the reality of God, and this world is framed in such a way that a supernatural being made it, and anything is possible to those who believe (see Mark 9:23).

"Now all wept and mourned for her; but He said, 'Do not weep; she is not dead, but sleeping.' And they ridiculed Him, knowing that she was dead.

"But He put them all outside, took her by the
hand and called, saying, 'Little girl, arise.' Then
her spirit returned, and she arose immediately."
(Luke 8:52-55)

By faith, we overcome, and by faith, we see miracles manifest. Things that were not, now are through trust and belief in the power of the living God moved by faith. I find it interesting that the Word of God states that things that are seen were not made from this world but a supernatural being who is invisible to our world. He has the power to speak this entire universe into existence. Is it that hard to believe He can raise a girl from the dead?

Now, I don't want to promote a blind faith; a lot of people can suggest that the Christian faith is blind. That is a naive blanket statement heard from sceptics and then believed to be a fact. Possibly this stems from misunderstanding John 20:29, but many who are not of the faith seem to think Christians just believe in a fantasy reality, but that's unbelief working in an unrepentant heart. The more we are open to Jesus, the more the Christian faith is made manifest to see the hand of God in everything.

Faith is not blind; it comes by hearing the word of God (see Romans 10:17). He is the author and finisher of our faith, after all. There is so much evidence of faith. Once we believe, we allow the Holy Spirit to teach and reveal to us. There are a few different types of faith that I will cover soon, but for now, let's look at the authority we have when the Word of God lands on the good soil of our hearts. In good stewardship and belief, we grow in grace by what Jesus did for us on the cross and the legal application that God ordained for us.

Jesus came to give us power, as He taught His disciples as one having authority to cast out demons (see Matthew 7:29). Jesus wants us to build on the foundations He laid. Just as the disciples, we also have authority. Not once in history did man have dominion over demons until Jesus came and taught with authority. He taught that we have authority in Christ, and that is where empowerment is found, by His blood and teachings. By His authority, we are His disciples. The Holy Spirit wants to teach us to be like Christ, who walked in this world.

First, I want to start with applying our discipleship because that's what I believe the Lord wants. He wants doers of His Word and for us to be learning to become disciples. Many people can debate if healing is for today. But it's often overlooked because of unbelief or not seeing results. There are many results in Christian groups who believe. When Jesus raised the girl from the dead, He only allowed those of His inner circle in the room, those who had hearts of belief and not scoffing or ridiculing mentalities, as others around Him had when He said the girl was not dead but asleep.

> "He permitted no one to go in except Peter, James, and John, and the father and mother of the girl."
>
> (Luke 8:51)

God still works miracles today, and He still equips ministers to lay on their hands in faith to expect healings. Part of serving Jesus is to exercise our spiritual giftings (see Romans 12:3-8). If we have our being in Him, we then have access to the supernatural healing power of His grace. We only need to believe that we have access to God's grace and His mercies will endure if we are trained and equipped in His ways and we understand the authority He has given us.

Suppose we look at the Old Testament and how God did many miracles and wonders. How much more favour do we have with the grace from Jesus at the right hand of the Father's throne? We are alive in Him, and we have our being held by His all-powerful hand. We have faith that can be given to us by the Holy Spirit. As we are abiding in the spiritual body of Jesus, we are in His power of life.

> "'In Him we live and move
> and have our being.'"
>
> (Acts 17:28)

Jesus is life when we are in fellowship with Christ. We have our very being shaped and energised by the power of God. Sometimes when I'm watching science documentaries about atoms, quarks and quantum physics, I see God's eternal power and how life down to the molecule was shaped and formed from the mouth of God. That is crazy to think about, yet true. We are formed from electricity, and the source of that power is given to us by God, who is light and life (see Genesis 2:7, Job 33:4, and John 1:3-4).

We have God, who is the life-giver. We are shaped into His image under His authority delegated to do good with love. We have an abiding right, a passport stamped by Jesus Christ. We have kingdom rights given to us just like when we have rights as citizens where we live now, we have kingdom rights to enter heaven through the blood of Jesus. We also have blessings we are entitled to by what Jesus did on the cross for us that are set in His Word as promises to be our provider, healer, salvation, joy, strength, source of peace, and that we will be heirs of the King of Kings. We have been given titles that are kings and priests before God.

> "To Him who loved us and washed us from
> our sins in His own blood and has made us kings
> and priests to His God and Father, to Him *be*
> glory and dominion forever and ever."
>
> (Revelation 1:5-6)

"But He *was* wounded for our transgressions,
He was bruised for our iniquities;
The chastisement for our peace *was* upon Him,
And by His stripes we are healed.
All we like sheep have gone astray;
We have turned, every one, to his own way;
And the LORD has laid on Him the iniquity of us all."

(Isaiah 53:5-6, emphasis added)

When Jesus died on the cross, He removed the curse of the law from us. When we were in our sins, the Bible talks about how the strength of sin is the law.

"The strength of sin *is* the law. But thanks *be* to God, who gives us the victory through our Lord Jesus Christ."

(1 Corinthians 15:56-57)

Since we were imperfect and under the law or moral law before Christ came, we now have overcome by our faith in Jesus Christ. Since we believe, we now have the right to victory over all the works of Satan, just as we have the right to salvation through faith.

As we just read, the prophet Isaiah was speaking the word of God boldly, declaring the blessing we are to inherit. Jesus was wounded for our sins. He was bruised for our unfair behaviour. He held the chastisement and endured it so we can have peace in this life. Even though we can be scattered and go our own ways, He still died for us to take all our burdens upon Him. This is His love. He paved a way for us to have faith in him. He has taken our sins and purchased us with the price of His sufferings for our peace and healing. By His stripes we are healed.

He endured pain and flesh being whipped off His body so that we can be healed. Past tense: as we believe in Him, we are saved by faith, we can trust and stand in the finished work of the cross. He has taken all diseases upon Him in His love toward us.

By the example He preached and walked out, Christ was teaching us a pattern that healing and miracles will happen by those who believe; Jesus said we will do greater works than He did.

> "'Most assuredly, I say to you, **he who believes in Me**, the works that I do he will do also; and **greater *works* than these he will do, because I go to My Father.** And whatever you ask in My name, that I will do, that the **Father** may be **glorified** in the **Son**. If you ask anything in My name, I will do *it*.'"
>
> (John 14:12-14, emphasis added)

Healing in the church serves our sovereign given rights as believers over the works of darkness. Secondly, healing adds to our testimonies of the supernatural power of God. His supreme authority and the substances of our faith are made known by our hope.

We have been given an unchangeable delegated authority in Jesus. His Word stays the same as He does not change. God has created a pattern for disciples to make more disciples. As we covered before, God doesn't change, but people do, paradigms do, and beliefs in what is possible often change. Let's have a quick detour into paradigms. It often takes just one person to change what is possible for the rest to follow.

Let's look at Roger Bannister, who was going to compete in a one-mile race. It was thought by experts such as doctors, sports trainers, and professional athletes that running a mile in less than four minutes was physically impossible for the human body to do. It was thought so impossible that no one could reach this goal. So as humans often do, we can set a belief to what is possible and what is not.

A mental barricade is often raised by people subconsciously that keep them within the beliefs of what can be done. But then one man defied the general paradigm and trained with passion and endurance to push the limits. Roger Bannister did not listen to the "experts" or the negative comments from people, but he rather pushed on into the unknown realm of pursuit.

At Oxford University at Iffley Road Track in Oxford in 1954, Roger competed in front of three thousand bystanders. He broke the "impossible" record with a time of **3:59.4**. People were amazed that the miracle mile was achieved.

The "impossible" was now possible! Since then, thousands have beaten the four-minute mark, and now it is considered the standard for high competing runners. We see it only took one person to break the standard paradigm, and then others believed it was possible and then achieved that time.

The current world record for one mile is 3:43.13, set by Hicham El Guerrouj of Morocco in 1999. In running terms, to be 17 seconds in front of the four-minute mark is enormous. Every millisecond counts in running, let alone seconds in the double digits! As humans, we see ourselves as conditioned by our environment and the general beliefs of what is possible. Jesus said that if we believe in our hearts, anything is possible.

Jesus came to this world to change how we understand what is possible. First, our salvation and the remission of sins can come through faith in the Son of God. He came to heal the sick and set the captives free who were oppressed by demonic powers. Jesus was teaching His disciples as one who has authority (see Matthew 7:29). Jesus was the visionary that linked newfound Christianity with power. He set the standards of what is possible in terms of discipleship and miracles. Naturally, if we have a leader like Jesus, who shows us what is possible through belief, we can break the four-minute mile spiritually.

God wants us not to listen to the paradigm of the world's beliefs, but rather make known the power of the Holy Spirit through demonstration and power (see 1 Corinthians 2:4). As we now know, the one-mile record has been absolutely smashed. God wants us to see the authority He has given us and to push past the unbelief in the world and church structures to reach "impossible" goals for His glory to be revealed and blessing to be abundant in the church.

We often see that Jesus trains His disciples and gives them an understanding of His power to walk with love and belief. First as to babes, He fed them simple truths and opened their hearts to believe. Often, He rebuked them because of their hardness of heart (see Mark 16:14 and Luke 9:41). Many can argue that healing is not for today because a lack of personal experience or being let down or not understanding the authority believers have and the spiritual warfare that is against Christians. There can be many reasons why many Christians can believe healing is not for today. Some teachings are against healing and some can think it was only for a time and a season, but in the right groups with people who walk in their spiritual giftings, Jesus is active and heals many through belief. I am not going to argue with unbelief: Jesus does not change. Still, people often look to sensationalism and search for miracles for man's glory and not God's, and that's possibly why many think healing has a bad reputation. There needs to be authenticity of heart toward God for His glory.

As the body of Jesus, we are not fully walking in the fruit of the spirit yet, let alone walking in the fullness of what Jesus wants to offer us. First, we need to be disciples trained and equipped in the word of truth, to activate the spiritual gifts and laying on of hands, and to receive impartation from the Holy Spirit from leaders who are walking in the truth and belief in God's ways. God will glorify His name, not man. He wants people to steward their gifts and walk in love first before authority is revealed in believers' lives. The Holy Spirit gives gifts to whom He wills (see 1 Corinthians 12:1-11).

> "'For he is sent by God. He speaks God's words,
> for God gives him the Spirit without limit.'"
>
> (John 3:34 NLT)

When we are walking as a disciple, God wants to trust us to obey Him and be good stewards of the giftings. To put it bluntly, many Christians in this world are either not seeking discipleship or exercising their faith in the spiritual gifts and do not believe it is possible for today; hence there is a lack of apostolic leadership in this modern age. Not Apostolic with the capital, rather lowercase, meaning not the twelve apostles ordained by God, but the five-fold ministry that the Holy Spirit taught the apostle Paul (see Ephesians 4:11-13).

Now I don't want to discourage anyone from discovering their spiritual gifts. You may not have a five-fold ministry. All ministries start from small beginnings (see Zechariah 4:10-14).

Jesus taught the disciples with smaller miracles first and opened their hearts to believe for bigger things like walking on water or raising the dead. We all have different giftings from the Holy Spirit, gifts of healing, miracles, prophecy, etc. God wants us to be like little children and believe what He has given us.

First, we must start taking baby steps as we endure, forge ahead with our faith, and start exercising our faith to put it into action. Just as muscles are exercised, we will grow more and more, but if we don't start, how do we expect to see any results? Anyone can simply start and pray for one another to lift one another up and expect to see people be healed.

It's faith that moves God, not man's qualifications. It's Jesus Christ who qualified us to start, and we need to build on what He has given us and run the race that He has set before us, to push the limits of society's paradigms and break records (so to speak). Jesus started healing fevers, which led to casting out demons and raising the dead. He was changing the beliefs of what was possible, and those who were following Jesus were opening their hearts to believe the fullness of the gospel to salvation.

I watched a video of a street evangelist laying hands on people in the streets and seeing people get out of wheelchairs and back problems being healed. He stated that he sees many miracles because he prays for many people. Not all receive healing, but many do. He said it took two years before he started seeing people being delivered consistently.

He persevered and stated his authority in the spiritual world in Christ. He was becoming a disciple of Jesus Christ, and Jesus promoted him when he was to be trusted as a faithful steward. Even though he had prayed for many people and did see street healings, it was a process and a journey Jesus was teaching him. That's not to say it's always that way, but God knows the heart and training necessary by the Holy Spirit. Jesus started, and He was the frontier that changed the way for people who did not know that there was healing in His name (see Mark 9:38-40). God gives giftings to those who are diligent in belief and are willing to step out in faith.

Jesus loves to heal people. He often does so and in many ways: He heals hearts, souls, minds, and lives, and blesses us with the hope that doesn't disappoint. I have often prayed for people when the opportunity arises, and it allows God to build my faith. One night I was having a friend over for an outdoor fire and BBQ, and he said to me, "Gosh, my shoulder is sore. It has been frozen for a few days now and I cannot move it." I said to him, "Can I pray for your shoulder?" He sort of believes in Jesus but was not fully aware of His realities. I said, "Let me do a short, simple prayer." He agreed, and I laid my hand on his shoulder. He went quiet and did not really talk much about it after I prayed. I did not want to push him and say, "How is it?"

After thirty minutes, I couldn't hold back my question and said, "I know Jesus healed your shoulder! How is it?" He said, "It's good!" And he started to happily demonstrate that he could now move it freely. It's funny sometimes the carnal understanding can be in shock from the supernatural and does not want to address it. But we see God was working in this situation. I had another guest who was there as well, but she did not believe. Twenty minutes after that, he was then proceeding to share what Jesus did for his shoulder and was revealing Jesus was real to this nonbeliever! As long as Jesus is glorified, we can step out and share God's truth and reality that He is always with us.

Another situation was when I was sharing the gospel with a young man who was going through a hard time. He did not necessarily believe it fully, but God was working in his heart.

I noticed he was holding his shoulder, and he said it was clicking and was causing pain for him. I just simply asked, "Can I pray for you?" He said, "Sure, why not!" As I prayed, he suddenly tried to move his shoulder in a full circle. He said, "It doesn't click anymore, and it does not hurt!" I said to the young man, "That's the power of Jesus, bro," and those seeds I'm sure will have an impact in his life. It's some of the ways God wants us to express our faith by stepping out like Peter did and was bold to share his faith and to believe to do the impossible!

Often, we do not see it because we do not try or persist. As God sees us to be faithful and have the correct motives for His glory and not our own, He will progress us to open our hearts from faith to faith! (See Romans 5:5).

Let's look at some biblical Scriptures that show us examples of His compassion and the physical healing that Jesus did.

> "Simon's wife's mother was sick with a high fever,
> and they made a request of Him concerning her.
> So He stood over her and rebuked the fever,
> and it left her. And immediately she arose."
>
> (Luke 4:38-39)

Here in the Bible, we see that this is one of the earliest healings when Jesus first started His ministry. Jesus was soon to rename Simon as "Peter," meaning "Rock." We understand that Jesus was revealing His healing power to His newly recruited disciples. He was teaching them and having compassion for all those He was around. Blessing was following Jesus everywhere He went. In those days, a high fever could be life-threatening before modern medicines and antibiotics. Jesus showed He has the power to heal, and He demonstrated His authority over Satan and diseases.

> "When the sun was setting, all those who had any that were
> sick with various diseases brought them to Him; and He laid
> His hands on every one of them and healed them. And
> demons also came out of many, crying out and saying,
> 'You are the Christ, the Son of God!'"
>
> (Luke 4:40-41)

This event was just after Jesus had healed Peter's mother-in-law. As she arose and was healed, she started to serve them with joy, having life back in her. However, after this event, word had gotten out among the local community of Capernaum.

Luke recounts that all who had diseases were coming to Jesus. He laid His hands on them, healing all of them and having compassion for the multitudes. We see that Jesus was exercising His authority to cast out demons who were oppressing these people. He showed examples that He is indeed the Christ by the authority to command demons to leave and be silent.

Before that time, the people of Israel did not have the authority to do so as we see later in the gospels how the Pharisees (the religious leaders) try to accuse Jesus of casting out demons because he is an evil ruler (see Luke 11:16-20) because He did things differently than them.

They used His compassion for people on the Sabbath as an accusation that He was evil because He was doing miracles in love rather than resting. Still, Jesus was showing God's heart to care for His people and to do good regardless of what day is meant for rest; mercy wins over judgment. God is good, and He wants us to mirror His approach of letting love reign in our hearts.

"A man who was full of leprosy saw Jesus; and he fell on *his* face and implored Him, saying, 'Lord, if You are willing, You can make me clean.'

"Then He put out *His* hand and touched him,
saying, 'I am willing; be cleansed.'
Immediately the leprosy left him."

(Luke 5:12-13)

When Jesus was travelling in between towns, many people came to Him as they heard the good news that there was a prophet in Israel. We can see the willingness of Jesus to heal when the leper said, "Are you willing?" This statement is for all of us to hear the faith that God wants us to have to ask, and yes, He is willing. He wants to heal us if we come to Him in faith and we believe He is a God who has mercy and compassion.

"I am willing," He said. Jesus was not afraid of the man with leprosy. In those times, lepers had to stand downwind from people to avoid giving others leprosy. It's interesting to see with some of the laws of God that one was to be kept cleansed, not to touch anything that would make one "unclean," but Jesus touched the man and healed him. This shows us that Jesus is the life-giver. Rather than the man with leprosy making Jesus unclean, it demonstrates that Jesus's power triumphs over all the works of darkness, and Christ's power is superior. What Jesus touches is made pure and is cleansed. It was not so in the Old Testament law. This shows us that Jesus was bringing in a new covenant that far supersedes the Old Testament law, and the power of His healing was to be increased to believers.

Expectant Faith

"And Jesus said, 'Who touched Me?'"

(Luke 8:45)

Faith has many ways of expressing itself. For example, if I was to say to my wife, "I trust you," that's quite a broad definition. Trust comes in many ways. I can trust her to be on time, I can trust her to do something I asked, or I can trust her to act in a manner that trusts me in a mutual agreement that has not necessarily been spoken about. A rapport has been established in our relationship. Well, Jesus's character of love establishes trust that He is good and has the power to heal. Faith comes by hearing, and there are many ways of hearing God. Jesus showed the reality of His power to the masses so much that it came to the point of belief that "if I just touch him, I will be healed."

A woman had been suffering for twelve years with a bleeding disorder, most likely from haemorrhaging polyps from her uterus that caused excessive amounts of bleeding. She required a miracle. She had spent all her money going to physicians, and her constant bleeding would have exhausted her body. The depletion of iron and other vital nutrients made her desperate just to touch Jesus's garment by pushing through the crowd pressing against Him. She said to herself, "If I just touch His garment's hem, I will be healed" (see Matthew 9:21). Her faith in touching Jesus's clothes led to an encounter that revealed it was not the clothes that Jesus was wearing that healed her, but rather the woman's faith in Him. She turned her eyes to Jesus, and He did not pray for her or even send His word to her; His healing came out of Him, and Jesus felt power leave Him. He quickly turned around and said, "Who touched me?" His disciples laughed and said there are many who are touching you. Jesus was talking to the person who had received healing from their faith, and He turned once the woman had confessed, and Jesus said, "Your faith had made you well" (see Matthew 9:22).

We see that Jesus does not always need to confirm with us His plans, but He responds to our faith and trust in His goodness. That is an expectant, moving faith. It's an example to us to seek Jesus's goodness for blessing and to have a rapport with His qualities of love and expect Him to heal.

There have many been past revivalists who have changed the way the believers look to Christ for healing mercies. For example, there have been some people God has used in a powerful way. "God's Generals" by Roberts Liardon is a great series on YouTube that documents past healing waves from the power of the Holy Spirit. Kathryn Kuhlman, Smith Wigglesworth, John G. Lake, and John Alexander Dowie are a few examples in the rich history of some more recent healing waves that allowed millions of people to come to faith in Christ.

The Welsh revival was one move of God that changed the paradigm for a lot of the other vanguards who followed suit later in the mid to late 1900s, where they were often in perilous times and during hardship of pandemics and famine that sparked desperation for God's Word to be believed and for the power of God to fall on blessed believers in Christ. [18]

Evan Roberts believed God for a harvest to start off the Welsh revival that saw 100,000 people come to faith in just a few months! [19] Where Christ was being preached, there was great expectation of His holy presence, and His love and mercies were shortly followed by miracles. Where the people grew for hunger and expectation, soon Jesus was the only name on everyone's minds.

> "'Anyone who believes and is baptized will be saved.
> But anyone who refuses to believe will be condemned.
> These miraculous signs will accompany those who believe:
> They will cast out demons in my name, and they
> will speak in new languages.'"
>
> (Mark 16:16-17 NLT)

Soon after Evan Roberts started preaching, crowds continued to flow in. It came to the point that the way of life started to change in the communities. The bars were empty, the judges wore white gloves because no murders or rapes or even small crimes were taking place in most parts of Wales. There had not been that occasion—well, basically never! Judges had no more jobs to undertake! We see revivals are not always about the signs and wonders, but a change in society. A change begins in the human heart, but

---

[18] "The Story of the 1904-1905 Welsh Revival," YouTube video, posted Nov. 15, 2019, https://www.youtube.com/watch?v=QfsDQ2QH0ZY

[19] Roberts Liardon, "God's Generals Series: Evan Roberts," YouTube video, posted March 26, 2020,
https://www.youtube.com/watch?v=8Jp85m6yl3s

signs will follow those who believe to confirm the gospel. Evan would often just wait at the altar and the Holy Spirit would come in like a zephyr wind, a gentle wind of the Spirit of God. Weeping would start, repentance of sins took place, hearts of unforgiveness would soon transition to love, and joy would be replaced. The power of the Holy Spirit soon cleansed the hearts of men and women.

There used to be many miners in Wales, and they would use donkeys to move the heavy loads out of the mines on the rails. The donkeys were so used to the swear words the men would speak to get the donkeys to start and stop the heavy loads. Soon, it became a hard task to operate the mines smoothly as the workers were so convicted about what they once said, they dared not use their old sayings. The donkeys had to be retired and new ones trained with polite words to start and stop. We see here it was a new way of life; the gospel brought people to know their sins, and then came the ecstatic joy of forgiveness from the grace of the Lord Jesus Christ.

People were seeking and expecting Jesus to heal, move, and work in the church. Workers would go straight from their jobs to church to try and get in to see what Jesus was going to do that night! No wonder the pubs were shut; no one wanted to drink nor have one drop near their tongues.

That is what Jesus does; He changes hearts to hunger for His ways of prosperity and peace and to expect a visit from the Holy Spirit in their midst. We can see a few years after this vivid explosion of salvations, it soon became apparent in a humble little street called Azusa. The move of the Spirit jumped over the pond, so to speak; hunger grew and testimonies could not be contained to just Wales, and that sparked world-wide momentum of great expectations of Christ to move with revivals and salvations that helped shape many people's hearts to know Jesus.

William J Seymour was leading the Azusa Street revival. [20] This small little town house soon boomed into people experiencing the miraculous, with the blind seeing, the deaf hearing, arms and limbs growing out that were once lost from defects or accidents, and massive amounts of people coming to know Christ. One of those was John G. Lake. He was involved in Azusa for a short time, and that led to a change in the way modern America understood practising medicine.

John G. Lake had healing rooms in Washington, D.C., and over a ten-year period, they had confirmed more than 250,000 were people healed from severe diseases and disabilities. Where people had no hope with doctors, John G. Lake's ministry taught people that Jesus gives healing like in the gospels. [21] John told the people coming to his rooms for prayer to go home for one month to read the gospels and to come back for prayer for healing. [22]We see the paradigm of belief was changed and new strides were made forward to the power of expecting the power of Jesus to come into their lives. These men and women who

---

[20] Roberts Liardon, "God's Generals Series: William J. Seymour," YouTube video, posted March 27, 2020, https://www.youtube.com/watch?v=gXti6tqkX9E

[21] "About John G. Lake," John G. Lake Ministries, https://www.jglm.org/john-g-lake/, Aug. 5, 2022

[22] Roberts Liardon, "God's Generals Series: John G. Lake," YouTube video, posted March 28, 2020, https://www.youtube.com/watch?v=__bKu8AzU3k

preached were trailblazers to be evangelists and to use the authority the Word of God gives believers to show the realities of Christ, back to a simple gospel of power and repentance to gain the attention of people and to lead them to the Cross of Calvary (see 1 Corinthians 2:1-5).

Gift of Faith

"So He said, 'Come.'"

(Matthew 14:29)

We see an example of a gift of faith when Peter asked Jesus, "Lord, if it is You, command me to come to You on the water" (Matthew 14:28). Jesus gave Peter confidence to step out onto the water. Jesus made it possible by His command to do so; it established the belief within Peter to be able to boldly step out of the rocking boat and land his feet on the rough seas that were splashing against the small fishing boat.

All things are possible to those who believe. It's essential to see that faith was met with a response: asking, "Lord, if it is you, allow me to come." Peter did not just run out onto the water, but he first inquired of Jesus. Peter was bold within that request when the other disciples may have been frightened for their lives and scared of the wild seas and chose to stay within the boat's safety.

Peter did the opposite; he ventured out into faith by joining Jesus. We see that the gift of faith given to Peter was an opportunistic faith rewarded by Peter's willingness to trust Him. Not every disciple was willing to trust Jesus with their lives in the middle of the Sea of Galilee. There were wild winds and rapid waves crashing against the boat. Peter went all in to meet his beloved Jesus, who was walking on water to guide them safely through the storm.

"'Yes, come,' Jesus said.

"So Peter went over the side of the boat and walked on the water toward Jesus. But when he saw the strong wind and the waves, he was terrified and began to sink. 'Save me, Lord!' he shouted.

"Jesus immediately reached out and grabbed him. 'You have so little faith,' Jesus said. 'Why did you doubt me?'

"When they climbed back into the boat, the wind stopped. Then the disciples worshiped him. 'You really are the Son of God!' they exclaimed."

(Matthew 14:29-33 NLT)

Peter, soon after walking on water, began to sink in the water because he was looking around at the situation of the storms, so he became frightened. Jesus gave him the rhema word in Greek, meaning "utterance." Jesus spoke the living words of faith, "Come," to empower him to step out.

He first started with assurance, but he allowed doubt to come in and the storm took his focus off Jesus. But Jesus never left him as he was sinking. Jesus came to him and immediately lifted Peter out of the water. Jesus never led Peter into danger. He was always there to show him His power and to help him when he doubted.

Jesus's lesson to His disciples was that He delivers and calms the storms and to have faith in His saving power. Jesus said to Peter, "You have little faith; why did you doubt?" We may think now, reading this verse, that it's a bit harsh to say he has little faith. He just walked on water! But it was the fact that he had the creator of the universe with him on the rough seas, and Peter was still afraid of the storm.

We can receive gifts of faith for the challenges in life when we are willing and ask Jesus for help. He wants us to respond by keeping our eyes directly on Him, so He can guide us to safe pastures.

Faith works in many ways, and there are so many different ways we can apply trust with Jesus, but some essential aspects to faith are asking, believing, waiting, and responding. Faith moves Jesus, and faith allows us to be empowered by His will and plans. It's a two-way street between knowing Jesus and receiving a gift of faith. As we move in His direction and show a willingness to trust Him, He can boost our trust in Him when He sees we are ready to respond.

I see this example of faith putting motion into the application. It reveals to us that all things are possible with God, and we should not limit Jesus. Instead, we should believe "He is a rewarder of those who diligently seek Him" Hebrews 11:6).

Faith allows us to overcome issues, and as we keep our eyes on Him and respond to His words, He gives us the confidence we need for this life journey over the rough seas. God gives faith to those who take His Word and are ready to use it. He works all things out for good in our lives and takes our hands if we doubt.

Many people can overcomplicate faith. Although there are different types of faith the Bible talks about, it's all one faith that leads to a substance that has value with God. The Bible talks about how our faith is more precious than gold (see 1 Peter 1:7). Faith is valuable, and genuine faith comes down to the amount we can place in Jesus.

If we think about how He created the vast universe and the world we live in, He has the key to it all, just like how a coder has a backdoor key to his design. Jesus has the key to doing things we do not have the code for, like walking on water, raising the dead, healing the deaf, making the blind see, and having victory over all diseases. Jesus's authority is everlasting, and His sacrifice on the cross enables us to place our trust and know His working power.

Jesus gives faith for us to believe, and He creates confidence. Sometimes people think we need to strive for belief, but that's not resting in the finished work and trusting God. That's taking matters into our own hands. We see that we can ask and be zealous like Peter and be ready to act, but if we are in Jesus and living in His vine, He will direct our desires and needs into His will for our lives. If we have the right heart, we will have the correct desires to bring forth fruitfulness and blessing. Always look to Jesus, trust His authority, and know He has it under control.

Great Faith

> "'I say to you. I have not found such great faith,
> not even in Israel!'"
>
> (Luke 7:9)

We see another example of Jesus's authority when a centurion who was a commander of the Roman army sent his servants to Jesus to ask for Jesus to heal his friend. As Jesus drew near the house, the Roman centurion sent word to Jesus, saying that the Roman was not worthy of talking to Jesus, let alone for Jesus to come under his roof. We see the reverence that the Roman commander had toward Jesus. Being from a different culture magnifies his faith that Jesus is worthy and that His words have power. The centurion said:

> "'Say the word, and my servant will be healed. For I also am
> a man placed under authority, having soldiers under me.
> And I say to one, "Go," and he goes; and to another,
> "Come," and he comes; and to my servant, "Do this," and
> he does *it*.'"
>
> (Luke 7:7-8)

Jesus marvelled at this man's faith and said that He had not even found faith like this in Israel. The friend of the centurion was healed that hour when they returned to the house. We see that faith in God and His Word reveal the importance of belief, and there is no limit to God. Jesus is inspired by faith because it shows we trust and understand that God is a good God who loves to give us the petitions we may ask of Him.

Great faith is not something unattainable; it is a simple understanding that Jesus has the authority to heal or whatever may be needed. Jesus applauded this man and sent word that his reverence and belief would be rewarded. Jesus then said that many will come and desire to come into the kingdom of heaven, but many will be left out through a lack of belief (see Luke 13:28). Jesus sees the heart, and it is the person's faith that shows if they are to inherit the kingdom of God, not if they are descendants of Abraham.

We see the love that Jesus was sharing with the commander. He was giving him a place high in honour because of his faith toward Jesus regardless of his background; his faith stood out and caused Jesus to marvel. The example was given to many around Jesus to share that faith is of the heart, and not even people in Israel had the faith of this man. It shows no boundaries to one who has a heart of belief and that how God rewards is unbiased to one's background or origin. He was an example for many of the gentiles to come to the faith of Christ, and Jesus was revealing this is great faith to act and respond in the way this man did!

CHAPTER 22

Be Still in Life's Storms

"O LORD my God, I cried out to You,
And You healed me."

(Psalm 30:2)

There are many testimonies of Christians sharing God's love and healing on 700 Club on YouTube channel. [23] Many people give their testimonies about how Jesus showed them His reality and how they received healing for their sicknesses. A young lady was sharing her testimony about when she had a tumour in her leg, but I'll come back to this testimony soon. This story goes well with resting in the boat in the storms of life.

On another occasion, before Peter walked on water, Jesus and His disciples were crossing the Sea of Galilee, and a great storm came against the boat; out of nowhere, the storm was furious. The twelve disciples were in fear and worrying about drowning. As panic set in, they started sweeping water out of their boat from the crashing waves.

Jesus was asleep at the back of the boat, resting His head on a pillow. As the twelve disciples saw Jesus sleeping there, they complained, "Lord, don't you care we are going to perish?" Jesus awoke and again said, "O you of little

---

[23] 700 Club Interactive, YouTube channel,
https://www.youtube.com/c/700ClubInteractive

faith?" He then rebuked the storm, and they marvelled, saying, "Who is this who can even calm the winds and sea?" (See Matthew 8:23-27).

We see Jesus was not fearful in the rough seas. He was asleep and resting while He understood that the Father was looking after Him. This is where some may say faith is blind, but not Jesus; He had a relationship with the Father and a rapport as we covered. He understood that the Father was going before Him and had trust in knowing God was going to work it out. Just because Jesus was resting does not mean He didn't care for the disciples. He did, but He allowed for their faith to grow.

He taught them to trust and be like Him and have the faith of a child depending on how His father was looking after them. God sees faith like a light shining up toward heaven. Salvation comes when one calls to God and admits their wrongs to Jesus. God listens and hears the cries. When one shows a sincere heart in calling out to God, the prayer sparkles and glistens to the Father's heart, and He receives the prayer petitions. God sees us (see Genesis 16:13). Looking to God and asking for His mercy to help allows faith to be birthed, and confidence grows. Jesus makes a way for us and intercedes on our behalf as our high priest.

When this young lady had a pain in her leg, she went to the doctor. [24] After a few tests, the report came back. The doctor said that they had found a tumour growing. This young lady said in her testimony that she did not worry. She was not frightened because Jesus was with her. Many

---

[24] Katie Woodward, "Testimony: God healed me from cancer!," YouTube video, n.d., https://www.youtube.com/watch?v=0hPJlRmh1ko&t=64s, Aug. 5, 2022

may panic like the twelve disciples in the boat. But she understood that resting in the storm was what Jesus wanted, as we have the Bible for learning and instructions so we can grow. She grew spiritually during her time in the Bible and knowing Jesus. Rapport is built over time, and faith comes by hearing the Word of God. As this lady was resting and not fazed by this terrible news, she trusted Jesus. When it was time for her to go back to the doctors for an updated scan, she had a peace that passed all understanding (see Philippians 4:6). The doctor said the lump had disappeared entirely. The doctor made a joke, saying maybe he had healing in his hands, but she smiled and said, "No, Jesus does."

"'I create the fruit of the lips:
Peace, peace to *him who* is far off and to
him who is near,' Says the LORD,
'And I will heal him.'"

(Isaiah 57:19)

"Be still, and know that I *am* God."

(Psalm 46:10)

" ' "Do not be afraid nor dismayed because of this great multitude, for the battle *is* not yours, but God's." ' "

(2 Chronicles 20:15)

The Bible shows us to have peace and to let God do the battles in whatever situation of life we have. If we place our simple faith in Jesus and wait for Him, it allows Him to work it all for our good. God is looking for His people simply to trust Him. There are no magic formulas or striving principles that achieve trust. Trust is within our hearts, and having a quiet and still kindness in the midst of life's storms is what shows confidence in God's abilities to deliver us.

We can have a still and calm inner peace, a peace that surpasses our logical understanding, and we can seek Jesus to comfort us. We can know we have Him with us in the boat, as Jesus allowed the disciples' faith to grow in that storm, but if you rest with Jesus, it makes it much easier, like how blissful it can be in the eye of the storm. God knows we can be in heartache and battles, but after all the trials, we will come out as purified and much more valuable than gold.

"In this you greatly rejoice, though now for a little while, if need be, you have been grieved by various trials, that the genuineness of your faith, *being* much more precious than gold that perishes, though it is tested by fire, may be found to praise, honor, and glory at the revelation of Jesus."

(1 Peter 1:6-7)

A faith that overcomes is a faith that can trust God amid challenging times when we don't understand all the situations and our logic can sometimes try to change our perspective of God's love. It's essential to have a stoic approach, as the apostle Paul did in his life's journeys. He was able to see past human suffering. He could see the glory that was transforming his life.

He was beaten, mocked, stoned to near death, despised by his fellow countrymen and rejected. He was in labour and working hard for Christ. Yet he was whipped nearly to death and beaten with rods three times; he was in constant danger from travelling in an outlaw time of the world. He was shipwrecked three times and left stranded without help and faced robbers greedy for gain and hatred from false brethren who tried to take him down. He often had nowhere to sleep and just had enough food and water to survive; he had constant troubles on his mind about the churches he had established and was sent a messenger, "a thorn in the flesh," to keep him from being puffed up with pride (see 2 Corinthians 11:25, 12:7).

His stoic understanding of reasoning from Jesus and seeking Christ's strength enabled him to keep his perspective of love pure. Rather than hatred and letting situations dictate what to believe by circumstances, he understood who Jesus Christ is and the riches we have in Him. Whether it's for a short period or a long period, we can be tested in trials to make sure our faith is genuine.

This allows us to see past our own biases and allow the Bible and a relationship with Jesus to reveal the truths, not to let our false concepts of pain and suffering change how we see Jesus and His truths shown in love. We are to look to the reward and a place in the kingdom that has been solidified for us to be in eternity with peace that unlocks the questions of life. It allows us to see with God's heart rather than our own understanding. When we come to the knowledge of Christ and are open to His teachings, it's like a domino effect that is set in motion. The way we can see the world changes, and it unlocks truths we never once saw because of our blinded understanding without Christ.

We see that our mentalities can shape us either with pride or humility, and one or the other affects what type of outcome we get. A flawed viewpoint on a situation can often lead to anger and a blur of understanding, yet a mindset of faith leads to peace and allows us to hear God's plans and purposes.

We are to look at what could have been without grace and mercy. How much worse would it be if God did not send His Son Jesus on the cross for us? There is much to be grateful for, and we should remind ourselves of the luxuries we have because of what Jesus has done for all of us if we allow Him. Having a humble mind will enable preconceptions to be diminished and gives way to a faith that leads to trust and fulfilment of joy.

> "To be carnally minded *is* death, but to
> be spiritually minded *is* life and peace."
>
> (Romans 8:6)

We are in control of what we allow ourselves to focus on. If we focus on questions we may never have answered in this life, it may lead to bad seeds being sown and allowed to germinate.

Once it starts growing, it can turn into anger and sin. But to sow seeds of trust and love in one's heart allows an intimate relationship with God and aspects of life to be changed for the good. It's not that we have blind faith; rather we have patience and allow God to change our view on how He sees things to be and how He is working things out for good. He will heal us by His grace and allow us to become fruitful in our spiritual growth. To see maturity coming out is to know a Christian that is not moved by what we see, but our hearts are moved by what God can do in our situations.

Apostle Paul said that when I am weak, I am strong; by allowing our fallen nature to die, we then come to the point of reliance on God. It draws us closer to Him spiritually when we understand our weaknesses.

When we are near Christ, we are naturally empowered by Him. When Moses spent forty days and forty nights with God while receiving the commandments, he ate no food and drank no water. God's glory was sustaining Moses. To our natural understanding, going without water for more than three days is impossible to survive; organs start to shut down.

God can do all things, and we are sustained in Christ as His glory is revealed in our lives. We have a helper, the Holy Spirit, who teaches us all things and He empowers us in times of need. We serve a supernatural God who gives strength when we are weak to make us strong. The heart that softly trusts Jesus is the heart that allows the power to come into one's life. God framed the world from His spoken words, and He can give us strength when we draw near to Him in full assurance of faith.

CHAPTER 23

To Fear Love

"The fear of the LORD *is* the
beginning of wisdom."

(Proverbs 9:10)

You may be asking, "Joel, why should we fear love?" But let me share a different perspective of fear. Biblical fear is a good thing. Sure, we can see fear as bad, but often fear is a mechanism for protection. How would we know not to put our hand in a fire unless we fear burning our hand? Fear can work both ways. Fear can give us wisdom in what choices to make.

God says the beginning of wisdom is the fear of God, when we have a holy, reverent fear of Him. Meaning when we fear God, we can come to the knowledge that He is the supreme ruler. By submitting, we can make wiser choices in the plans and paths He has for us. Love is all powerful and having a godly fear is for our safety. When we understand that God is called love, we can place our trust in Him to look after us and let Him make the decisions. When we release our conclusions unto God and allow Him to take our burdens, we are saying, "Ok God, I trust you. I want you to work everything out in my life for my good. I am committing my life into your hands." When we know that He sees all the different paths we can take and the different obstacles in our way, we can either say, "I'll do it my own way and learn from my own understanding and be out of the protection of the ship," or we can say, "I'll fear you and trust that what you have for me is in my best interest for this life and the one to come."

We need to be humble and learn to fear Him to know His ways. At the start of this book, we went over His creation, and we understood just a small aspect of His creative powers. When we understand the magnitude of the Earth and all the beautiful creations, not to mention the universe, He deserves to be feared with holy awe, wonder, and amazement. If we don't do that, are we acting in humility? How can we expect to grow if we don't recognise He is far beyond our understanding and wisdom?

We can see a reasonably healthy fear that keeps our feet steady on His knowledge and mercy as we understand these truths. God wants us to know that to fear Him is pleasant; we see in Psalm 119 that a godly fear brings delight, safety, and joy.

"How can a young man cleanse his way?
By taking heed according to Your word.
With my whole heart I have sought You;
Oh, let me not wander from Your commandments!
Your word I have hidden in my heart,
That I might not sin against You.
Blessed *are* You, O LORD!
Teach me Your statutes.
With my lips I have declared
All the judgments of Your mouth.
I have rejoiced in the way of Your testimonies,

As much as in all riches.
I will meditate on Your precepts,
And contemplate Your ways.
I will delight myself in Your statutes;
I will not forget Your word.

ℷGIMEL
"Deal bountifully with Your servant,
That I may live and keep Your word.
Open my eyes, that I may see
Wondrous things from Your law.
I *am* a stranger in the earth;
Do not hide Your commandments from me.
My soul breaks with longing
For Your judgments at all times.
You rebuke the proud—the cursed,
Who stray from Your commandments.
Remove from me reproach and contempt,
For I have kept Your testimonies.
Princes also sit *and* speak against me,
But Your servant meditates on Your statutes.
Your testimonies also *are* my delight
And my counselors."

(Psalm 119:9-24, emphasis added)

"Open my eyes." Poetically, the psalmist is declaring God's unfailing love to those who fear Him. We see wisdom brought to life as a light bulb emitting from the psalmist's heart. God is our counsellor. When we first understand that we can learn to grow in His grace and when we meditate on His goodness and the faithfulness of His law, it brings forth fruitful living and a new identity in wanting to please Him. To seek righteousness is just!

Wonderous things come from godly fear. It allows God's favour! Meditating on His Word will enable us to have a fear that God cares for us and is faithful. God's faithfulness is like a roaring lion that protects its young or like a mother bear over its cubs. The testimonies of the patriarchs in the Bible reveal and impart God's strength to us and can give us the faith into our hearts to Trust Him. When we search after God's qualities, faith and wisdom will be given to us the more we immerse our minds into God's past faithful acts of people's faith and triumphs!

The psalmist was saying he delights in knowing the knowledge of God. The Bible has a lot to say about wisdom, and it all comes back to fearing God. The Bible covers gold, jewels and their values, but in it all, nothing compares to wisdom. This is the fear of the Lord that will result in true riches. If we fear Him, we are safe and protected under His wings. To have His grace and favour is the best blessing of all. Job understood a few things about suffering. He went through tribulations and trials like not many others. He gained wisdom in his trials and understood that the greatest things in life were not about what he had but whom he had relationships with.

> " ' "Behold, the fear of the Lord, that *is* wisdom,
> And to depart from evil *is* understanding." ' "
>
> (Job 28:28)

Job was a wealthy man and was prospering in life until God allowed Job to go through suffering. In these great sorrows,

Job suffered much, but wisdom and riches were brought out in his life spiritually. The book Job authored taught us the actual value of who God is and what is the meaning of life. There can be much we can gain in this world, but if we do not acknowledge God, it will ultimately be worthless and have no eternal value. To fear God is to know liberty, love, joy, and the relevance of lasting rewards.

> "'Do not fear those who kill the body but cannot
> kill the soul. But rather fear Him who is able to
> destroy both soul and body in hell.'"
>
> (Matthew 10:28)

God never wanted to send anyone to Hell, but with wickedness, they must be judged, and if we do not allow God to show us His true love, how can we hear if we fail to listen? How can we be ready to hear rebuke if we are not willing? We must fear the power that is able to cast us into hell. I think that is the best start to understanding that fear is reasonable.

To have a holy fear shows us two alternatives: one is an eternal home with rewards and blessings, while the other is disobedience to God, He who upholds the standard of righteousness. To be disobedient to love is agreeing with evil and saying we are more righteous than God. To have that mindset shows us that we do not want to change our ways, and God has no option other than sending all of those who refuse to believe the truth to hell. You may say, "Joel, how is that love?" At the start of the book, we covered some of these issues, but in fairness, many people want these questions answered. We can have our eyes covered by our own moral understanding, but that does not mean that it is correct. We see evil every day. We can allow society to dictate and push ethical boundaries all the time.

We must understand that our perceptions of evil and sin do not always equal the standard of God's holy goodness. To understand the moral law that He has set within our hearts, we first must be able to take notice of His commands. If we (humans) fail to listen to God, He can allow non-believers to decline into moral decay. You may say, "Why would He allow non-believers to not believe and cast them aside and allow them to be put over to a depraved mind?"

"Since they thought it foolish to acknowledge God, he abandoned them to their foolish thinking and let them do things that should never be done. Their lives became full of every kind of wickedness, sin, greed, hate, envy, murder, quarrelling, deception, malicious behaviour, and gossip. They are backstabbers, haters of God, insolent, proud, and boastful. They invent new ways of sinning, and they disobey their parents. They refuse to understand, break their promises, are heartless, and have no mercy. They know God's justice requires that those who do these things deserve to die, yet they do them anyway. Worse yet, they encourage others to do them, too."

(Romans 1:28-32 NLT)

It's because they keep resisting the Holy Spirit and constantly reject God's truths. God is holy and righteous, and if people refuse the gospel and they will not be saved, it is much better for them to be blinded, lest they are convicted heavily for great transgressions if they did first believe then reject the truth. We see even God is merciful to sinners who reject the gospel of love. Just like when Jesus said:

"'Seeing they may see and not perceive,
And hearing they may hear and not understand;
Lest they should turn,
And *their* sins be forgiven them.'"

(Mark 4:12)

Jesus has stated clearly that He wants all to turn from their sins and repent so He can forgive them (see 2 Peter 3:9), but He is also teaching it is for their protection that if they do believe and then reject the gospel, it would be much worse for them to walk over the cross and put Christ to shame (see Hebrews 6:6).

We all have choices in this life. One is to fear God and heed rebuke because the Bible says whom He rebukes is whom He loves! If we fail to listen to God, He gives us the consequences of not wanting to hear. He shares that it is appointed once to death, then the judgment. Failing to understand those fundamental principles will reveal a stubborn heart and a heart that prefers to choose sin over love.

Since we are created to be immortal after death, our spirit must go somewhere. Suppose you do not belong to Jesus Christ by faith and belief. The devil wants to take you to hell legally. Because God cannot protect you, you are under the law and not grace; since the strength of sin is

God's law, we must understand we have all broken His commands and chosen to practise sin.

There must be a removal of that sin to enter into heaven to be able to live with God. Without us having faith and remission of sin and believing that Jesus was the removal of sin for us, God's son who was rejected in turn leaves God to judge because you may have disregarded the gospel (if you are not a believer).

"The sting of death *is* sin, and the strength of sin *is* the law.
But thanks *be* to God, who gives us the
victory through our Lord Jesus Christ."
(1 Corinthians 15:56-57)

We see then that knowledge can give us a fear that can save our souls by repenting of our sins and asking for Jesus to provide us with eternal hope with Him. In heaven, there are no diseases, no decay, no injustice. It will all be made right. Whatever wrongs we have experienced in this life will soon be forgotten, for the wonderful eternal life will begin.

If you are not a Christian and have come this far without accepting Jesus Christ to live within you, I urge you to consider doing so. You have everything to gain, but if you reject the gospel, you will lose everything after this life. It's simple: God is always with us; He is always around us. He knows all events. That's who He is! He will forgive you if you simply ask for forgiveness of your past sins and ask Him to come and give you a new spiritual heart of love! Your journey will start from there. I suggest you find fellowship with Christian communities who can help your journey and enjoy other like-minded people who can direct you into deeper biblical truths.

Many wonder if God is love, why do bad things happen? God never promised for us not to have bad things happen. It is a part of living in a decaying world that is full of sin. We all have fallen short of God's holiness and allowed the devil to be a ruler in this world, but that's where the love of God has come in. People are regularly blindsided by this fact. Jesus did come to share His truth, what He has done, and how He has dealt with sin if we trust Him.

He taught us that there would be tribulations in this life, but we have hope that will endure through it. We have rewards and gifts of happiness that are to come! We can be a part of His family and be under His protection, away from the devil and his demons. We will find a place to call home and a reality will be formed; as we have experienced this world, we will share the next one.

Many can be taken young, and many can live to old age. I spoke to a man who used to be a Christian until his grandpa died from cancer. He stated that if God were real, He wouldn't let that happen. His grandpa was a Christian and lived a good life. My heart began to fill up with love and compassion for this man. It is a question I have often had presented to me, and sometimes it's different forms of questions of "why do bad things happen?" Many can stumble on this question that can rob them of a relationship with God.

The devil's tactic is to divert and direct anger toward our maker. We do not know how this Earth was made or how the planets or stars were formed. God does, and He has a lot more understanding than we do. Some questions we don't have all the answers to, but I think there will be very good, reasonable answers once we get to heaven and ask Jesus, and I think we will be surprised at the answers given to us by God and the right decisions He has made. Not that we should ever expect Him to give sufferings to us, but He will reveal His heart and why there had to be suffering. We know some questions, and with much reasonable thought, there are always answers, but sometimes we can be biased toward them because of our hurts.

This is not judging this man's faith, but it shows us how a lack of understanding or development can allow the devil to try and rob us of Jesus's love by leaning on our own understanding of why bad things happen. I understand bad things happen, but we don't always see what God sees; here's a biblical perspective of God's view and not ours.

"The righteous perishes,
And no man takes *it* to heart;
Merciful men *are* taken away,
While no one considers
That the righteous is taken away from evil.
He shall enter into peace;
They shall rest in their beds,
Each one walking *in* his uprightness."

(Isaiah 57:1-2, emphasis added)

This man could know that his grandpa went to a better place; he was taken away from evil, a place that has no pain. He was able to see the Father, Jesus, and the Holy Spirit! To experience God's heaven with inexpressible joy! His grandpa would not want him to be angry at God; rather trust that God was working it out for good.

It's vital to have roots developed in our hearts that last in hard times. This life can be unfair; it does not mean God will allow His children to be put to shame. We must understand God's ways are not always our ways. But we mustn't question God's hand. Because He is the one who gives us life, and what we may have in this world is because God gave it to us first (see Job 1:21). He can take it away if He wills, not that He takes life, but sin does by allowing death into this world. Now I am not saying sin is why this man's grandpa became ill, not at all. But in this life, there is an adversary, the devil.

"The thief does not come except to steal, and to kill,
and to destroy. I have come that they may have life,
and that they may have *it* more abundantly."

(John 10:10)

The devil is often skilful and shifts the blame toward God to try and get people to question God and His love. But in fairness, we need to take responsibility for our actions and see that the devil is the one who destroys people's lives.

Jesus has come to give us life and life more abundantly. We can see God's ways of working all things for good in our lives through belief and patience, even if we don't understand why bad things can happen. We must know that there is a war that we cannot see, and there is a spiritual war ground that the devil can try to use to bring harm to people. He wants to break up families. Jesus said many people hear His words, but when trials come, the devil takes away the seeds that God has sown.

"'These are the ones by the wayside where the word is sown. When they hear, Satan comes immediately and takes away the word that was sown in their hearts. These likewise are the ones sown on stony ground who, when they hear the word, immediately receive it with gladness; and they have no root in themselves, and so endure only for a time. Afterward, when tribulation or persecution arises for the word's sake, immediately they stumble.'"

(Mark 4:15-17)

These are questions in life we all have. We have all been affected by death, but this is where the love of God shows us His workings. In many ways, people see the end as inescapable and true. But Jesus has overcome death, and if we are in Him with belief, we will be saved from the second death (hell), which lasts forever. Simply ignoring hell does not make it cease to exist. One who can allow God's truths to enter on good soil will see that being naive does not keep us from judgment. Acknowledging God and becoming humble will allow the hurts to be healed in our lives by accepting the goodness that God has offered us by His sacrifice on the cross.

To fear God is to choose the right path regardless of outcomes. As we have covered with the devil and his demons, they will be cast into the lake of fire for eternity. Day and night, they will be tormented for the wickedness they have inflicted on humankind.

There will be all wrongs made right when God judges. God has His timing with it all. And in His longsuffering and patience, He is waiting for everyone to have opportunities to turn from their sins before He wraps up this age and ushers in the new heaven. Be wise and choose eternal security over the fleeting pursuit of our heaven on earth.

God made us to be in fellowship with us. To love us and to have a rewarding relationship. He gave us a will to choose, and He wants us to choose love over death. It shows us that our human condition, the fallen nature, and the ruler of this world can be so deceiving that it can often deceive us into choosing death instead of life.

"'For whoever finds me [wisdom] finds life,
And obtains favor from the LORD;
But he who sins against me wrongs his own soul;
All those who hate me love death.'"

(Proverbs 8:35-36)

"All those who hate me love death." What a powerful statement that is. People often hate God without realising they are in agreement with death. We see people who love skulls, death, violence, and more. It shows a lifestyle that conflicts with holiness. It reveals the character of those who love to sin. People can see death as being cool until it happens to them or their loved ones. There is nothing cool about death, loss, and tragedy. The devil is a deceiver and the father of lies (see John 8:44). If he can try to make sin "cool," he will and does. If he can try to create honour among death, he does it with vanity through lies and deceit. He tries to break families apart and destroy them. We are made in the image of God. He hates God and tries to hurt God by deceiving us and blindfolding us into loving death.

> "[The gospel] is veiled to those who are perishing, whose minds the god of this age has blinded, who do not believe, lest the light of the gospel of the glory of Christ, who is the image of God, should shine on them."
>
> (2 Corinthians 4:3-4)

I know talking about the devil can seem out there for some, but it's the truth. We must understand that there is an adversary. We cannot be naive about why there is pain and death in this world. Instead of showing anger toward God, we must gain understanding to see the root of the issue. We have been given authority in this world, and sin can try to take away the power God has given us. We have been given the gift of life, but we can sometimes turn our fist at God and allow the devil to try and keep us in captivity.

That's why Jesus said He has come for the broken-hearted and to set the captives free. With sin being dealt with, we have new life, and new liberties are to be used and declared to stand and see victory. We are more than overcomers through Jesus. He opens the eyes of the blind and heals the hearts of many. Instead of blame-shifting, we need to use our authority in Christ and not tolerate the devil to see God's intended plans.

> "For I know the thoughts that I think toward you, says the LORD, thoughts of peace and not of evil, to give you a future and a hope. Then you will call upon Me and go and pray to Me, and I will listen to you."
>
> (Jeremiah 29:11-12)

Did you know that God knows the very hairs on your head? (See Matthew 10:30.) This is the God who cares so intimately for us to give us hope and an expected end. He gave us His son for the propitiation of our sins, as He said.

"'O Death, where *is* your sting?
O Hades, where *is* your victory?'"

(1 Corinthians 15:55)

The true gospel is victory over death, defeating the second death, and being made as a new creation. We see two worlds working when the gospel frees us while the devil tries to blind and entrap God's creation through various ways of pleasure in this life.

To fear love is the best approach: fearing God brings about blessing, while sin leads to death and dishonour. My heart goes out to people who think death is cool. We see it is stale, lifeless, and rotting. That is not a place fit for people who are made in the image of God, as we can see God's love does equal Jesus in us. He only wants to bring joy into our midst, but as humans, we often only search for the beauty in life after it's gone or when we go without. Now we are to be wise and grab hold of eternal life now and allow the love of the gospel to reach as many as it can before Jesus comes back to set in order the Lord's day of righteousness and judgment.

Thank you for reading *Jesus Equals Love*.

If you have enjoyed this book, please leave a review of what you have liked so others can be blessed and be encouraged by choosing to read it. Please if led to do so, leave positive rating as this really blesses me greatly to help share this message of God's love!

Thanks,
Joel Wright